Understanding Buses

Second Edition

Chris Cheek

Published by Passenger Transport Intelligence Services Limited (PTIS)
83 Latimer Road, Eastbourne, East Sussex BN22 7EL
Telephone: 01729 840756
E-mail: info@passtrans.co.uk
Web: www.passtrans.co.uk

ISBN 978-1-898758-19-8

© Passenger Transport Intelligence Services Limited 2019-2021

All rights reserved. No part of this publication may be used, reproduced or transmitted in any form by any means electronic or mechanical, including the photocopying, recording or by an information storage and retrieval system, without prior permission in writing from the publisher.

Author: **Chris Cheek BA FCILT MCMI**

First Edition: January 2019
Second Edition: May 2021

Cover Illustration: shows one of the electric double deckers entering service in London and around the country, manufactured by Alexander-Dennis and BYD. Courtesy of Alexander Dennis Ltd.

Contents

Bus Industry Costs 11
    Overview 11
    The Components of Cost 11
    The Primary Drivers of Cost 15
    Calculating the Resources Needed 16
    How much does it cost? 19

Trends in Unit Costs 21
    Labour 21
    Other Costs.. 23
    Summary... 27

Bus Industry Profits 29
    Introduction 29
    Raising capital – the creation of obligations 29
    How much profit?.. 30
    Profits earned.. 37
    Overall Conclusions 38

Demand for Bus Services 41
    What drives demand?.. 41
    Overall Volumes of Travel.. 43
    Why Volume Matters 46

Population 47
    Introduction 47
    Population Density 47
    Age and Gender 49
    Socio-Economic Groups... 51
    Access to Cars 52

Journey Purpose 55

Introduction	55
Analysis Tools	55
The Relative Importance of Each Purpose	55
Changes in Journey Purpose	57
The Bus Product	**59**
Overview	59
Getting to the Bus Stop	60
Waiting for the Bus	60
On the Bus	61
Price	63
Quality	63
Putting it Altogether	64
How Generalised Cost works	65
Understanding the Effect of Change	69
Keeping the Customer Satisfied	**71**
Introduction	71
What Customers Want	72
Meeting Customer Requirements	75
Customer Information and Communication	79
Conclusion: Customers at the Heart of the Business	83
Competition	**85**
Overview	85
The Demographic Challenge	85
External Competition	86
Conclusions on External Competition	88
Internal Competition – Other Bus Services	89
Fares and Ticketing	**93**
How fares are determined	93
How Fares are Set	98

Drivers of Fare Changes 99
Tracking Fare Levels 100
Average Revenue per Passenger Journey 100
Comparative Travel Costs 104
Concessionary Travel 106

Public Spending on Bus Services 111
Overview 111
The Purpose of the Spending 111
Benchmarking Spending 114
Changes in Spending Patterns 116

Looking Ahead 117
Covid-19 and the Future 117
De-carbonising Transport 120
Conclusions 123

About the Author

Chris Cheek has worked in the public transport industry for over 48 years, the last 33 as an analyst and consultant.

He started his career with the National Bus Company in 1972 and held several line management posts in bus operations, coaching and tourism marketing.

He has worked on a wide variety of projects including seven passenger rail franchise bids and more than ten PFI bids for rapid transit projects in the UK and overseas. He has worked with all the major transport groups on a range of projects and with the UK and devolved governments. He also advised lenders and City institutions on acquisitions and flotations. He has appeared as an expert witness in two public inquiries and speaks regularly at conferences and seminars.

Since 1991, he has edited major research publications on public transport, including *Rail Industry Monitor*, *Rapid Transit Monitor*, *Bus Industry Monitor* and *Concessionary Fares UK*. He now edits the *Passenger Transport Monitor*, the online subscription service that replaced the industry monitor publications in December 2009.

He is a regular contributor to the trade press and helped to found *Passenger Transport* magazine. He also helped to found two schemes designed to promote excellence and good practice in the industry, the UK Bus Awards and the UK Coach Awards.

Chris has also published five novels, *The Stamp of Nature* (June 2018), *A Year of Awakening* (October 2018), *Veering Off Course* (February 2019), *Governing Passions* (June 2020) and *Setting a New Course* (March 2021). He writes regular blogs at www.chrischeek.me and www.passtrans.co.uk/blog

Chris is a Fellow of the Chartered Institute of Logistics and Transport and a Member of the Chartered Management Institute.

Preface to the First Edition

For a whole variety of reasons, the bus industry continues to be of vital importance to the UK. It remains central to the economy, to plans to combat climate change and pollution, and to policies regarding social inclusion and accessibility. Since 2012, research undertaken for Greener Journeys[1] in a series of reports by KPMG and the University of Leeds has demonstrated the size of the contribution the industry makes to the overall economy, including:

- 170,000 jobs plus another 83,000 jobs in the supply chain
- £64 billion of GVA contributed by bus commuters
- £27 billion worth of retail activity by bus passengers
- £6.2 billion worth of leisure spending by bus passengers

The industry carries more than 2.2 million people to work and back every day, accounting for up to 14% of all commuting in some areas[2].

Yet, public and political comment on the industry continues to betray a lack of understanding and, it often seems, a degree of prejudice. Politicians who say that they are pro-bus, are often highly critical of bus services in Council meetings and in the media - often without much (or any) justification, and certainly without understanding of the complex issues involved. The problem is that such ill-informed comment constantly reinforces the choice that the car commuter made.

At central government level, policy towards the industry has a crucial effect on the long term investment decisions which operators must make, and national statements by ministers can affect decisions just as much as factors in the local market. Taxation is a key issue here: bus travel is the only form of public transport that pays significant levels of tax on its fuel: relief was offered for many years in the form of Fuel Duty Rebate (renamed Bus Service Operators' Grant, or BSOG for short, in 2000).

---

[1] *For the full range of Greener Journeys research reports on the economic benefits of the bus, and of investing in bus infrastructure, please see* https://greenerjourneys.com/keywords/economic/

[2] *PTIS analysis of Transport Statistics Great Britain, Sheet TSGB0108.*

However, it has since been cut and whittled away in other ways, whilst its abolition is canvassed by the Treasury during every comprehensive spending review. This causes further anxiety and uncertainty.

This approach has to be contrasted with the approach to fuel duty for motorists, which has remained virtually unchanged since the turn of the century, as politicians remain frozen by the headlights of the fuel tax rebellion of the late 1990s. In the absence of road pricing, fuel taxation is the only way that government can use the tax system to change behaviour to reduce congestion and pollution. It is admittedly a blunt instrument, but if Ministers are not prepared to use it, they should find better ones.

I have long argued that the industry is not as good at putting its own case across as it should be. It is one of the reasons that I got involved in monitoring and tracking the industry in the *Bus Industry Monitor* project in the first place. It is also why I, along with colleagues, helped to found the UK Bus Awards in 1996.

Through work on the Monitor project, I have been studying the industry for some 30 years, working with colleagues and clients all over the country and attempting to understand the trends and what drives them.

Since 2010, the industry has undergone another period of huge change, coping with cuts of more than 27% in public spending against the background of increasing congestion, difficult economic circumstances and huge social and economic change driven by the smartphone and internet revolution.

In recent speaking engagements I have tried to communicate to audiences of non-specialists how these things are all inter-related and happen against the background of the financial realities of trying to run a successful bus operation. These challenges are not about regulation or ownership, but about how to deliver successful and sustainable bus services to the millions and millions of people who rely on them every day.

This book is designed to take that message a stage further, to offer a clear, non-technical, jargon-free explanation of how the bus industry works.

In the chapters that follow, I examine:

- The costs of operation – what the components are and what drives them, particularly understanding the crucial importance of speed and predictability
- The revenue earned – how much is needed to enable operators to meet their three key objectives:
  - to cover their costs
  - to meet their financial obligations
  - to invest in the future
- The need for profit – why operators need to make a surplus and what they do with it
- The principal drivers of demand for bus services
- The bus product – its various attributes and why they are important

The competitive environment in which the industry operates
- Trends in fares and ticketing
- Public spending on buses

It is not now and never has been the purpose of my work to provide public policy solutions, merely to try to ensure that the facts of a situation are known and understood before such judgements are made. I hope and believe that this book follows in that tradition. As with our other reports under the *Passenger Transport Monitor* banner, this book, and the research which goes with it, was undertaken as part of the company's normal commercial activities and has not been funded in any way by any third party.

Chris Cheek BA FCILT MCMI
Passenger Transport Intelligence Services Limited
January 2019

Preface to the Second Edition

This second edition of *Understanding Buses* has been produced with three objectives in mind: firstly, to update some of the data contained in the charts and tables; secondly, to reflect some of the important changes in costs that have taken place since the original was prepared three years ago; and thirdly to incorporate some analysis of the likely effect of the Covid-19 pandemic on the industry.

Much of the text remains unaltered from the first edition. This is deliberate, since much of the book is about the principles that underlie how the industry works and the best practice that is adopted in putting them into effect. I was also conscious that readers had praised the clarity of the explanations and the lack of jargon, and I was keen to maintain this.

I did feel it important that the data used in the worked examples and other analysis should be as up to date as possible - most figures are now from the 2018/19 financial year, which will be the last genuinely "Covid-free" period. It will thus come to be regarded as the last year of the old regime, and also the base from which future trends are likely to be judged.

Recent events are discussed, albeit briefly, in an expanded Chapter 12 - which looks at the consequences for the industry of Covid-19 and government policy changes, as set out in Decarbonising Transport agenda published in March 2020 and the National Bus Strategy a year later. It is of course far too soon to say how any of these major changes are going to play out.

In the end, though, all those effects and policies will work through *within* the framework of the economic, financial and human constraints in which the industry works. It seems to me that an understanding of that framework and its constraints is essential for planners, policymakers and other stakeholders - and that is what this book sets out to provide.

Chris Cheek BA FCILT MCMI
Passenger Transport Intelligence Services Limited
May 2021

1
Bus Industry Costs

Overview

Essentially, bus industry costs are a function of three elements:
- The level of service
- Input prices
- Asset utilisation

The level of service – where routes go, how quickly and how often – is the key factor in driving industry costs. It is typically measured and benchmarked by the number of miles operated. As we shall see, though, most industry costs are time-based, so that a measure of the number of hours the bus operates ("bus hours") is more useful for costing purposes.

Input prices determine unit costs for day-to-day items such as wages, fuel and spare parts and indeed the vehicles themselves. In turn, the cost of vehicles will influence the amount of capital employed to run the business and the cost of financing that.

Asset utilisation is driven by the industry's ability to use its resources wisely and efficiently; this is primarily a function of the speed at which buses can operate and the predictability of the journey time. If buses go more slowly, because of traffic congestion for example, then more vehicles and more drivers will be required to deliver the same level of service, so pushing costs higher.

In this chapter, we will examine these issues in more detail and provide worked examples of some of the key concepts.

The Components of Cost

The costs of operating bus services can be divided into six major components, which are:
- Labour
- Fuel
- Overheads

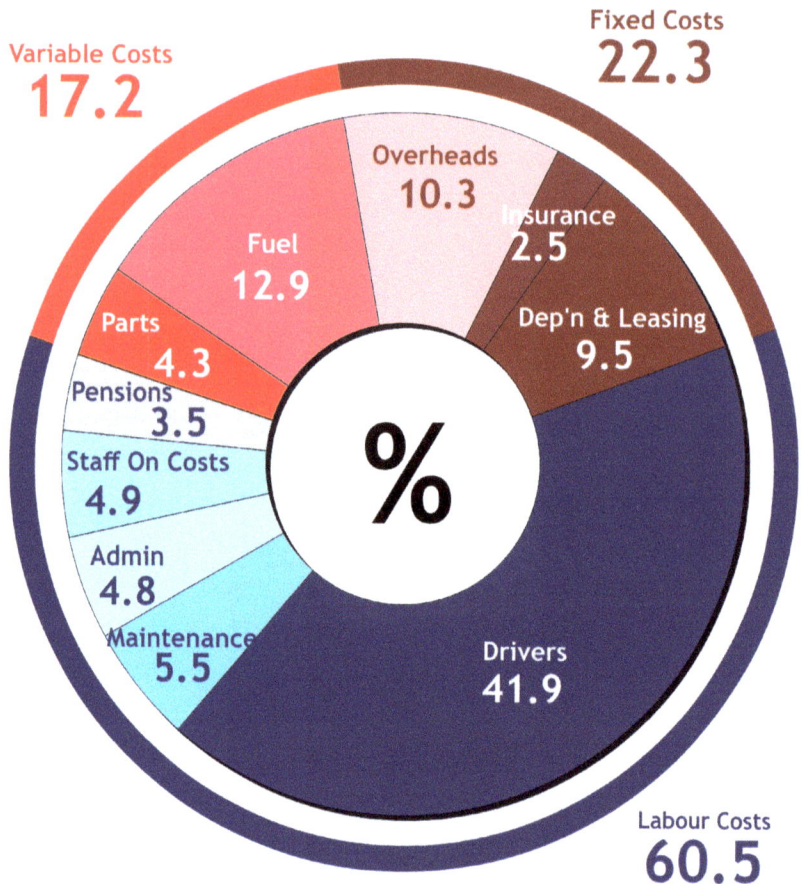

Figure 1-1: Breakdown of Bus Industry Costs, 2020

Source: PTIS Bus Industry Monitor database

- The cost of the equipment required (charged as depreciation for owned assets and/or leasing charges where operating leases are used)
- Bus maintenance materials
- Insurance

The approximate breakdown of these major components in 2017 is shown in Figure 1-1 above.

Labour Costs

Bus driver wages are the single largest component of costs, accounting for almost 42% of the total. The wages and salaries of other staff – required for maintenance, administration and supervision – account for a further 10.3%. Then there is the cost of pensions, social security, and other employee benefits. Labour therefore accounts for over 60% of the total.

Fuel

Fuel costs have accounted for an increasing proportion of the total in recent years because of changes in price and taxation

Fuel costs are driven by four factors:
- Fuel prices
- Fuel efficiency
- Scheduled speed and congestion levels
- Government taxation policy.

Overheads (including Administration)

Overheads include costs such as administration, supervision, and properties. Information technology and other changes in administrative practice have had a huge effect in recent years.

Overhead costs will be driven by:
- the numbers of managers and supervisors
- the costs of utilities
- waste disposal costs
- staff salaries
- rents, property costs, land values and business rates.

Bus Maintenance

As the cost of the maintenance staff has already been covered under 'labour' above, these costs relate mainly to the tools needed and the spare parts required. The industry has made major savings in maintenance costs over the last 25 years, as the reliability of vehicles and components has improved, and new technology has been introduced.

As a result, the life of major units such as engines and gearboxes, as well as other smaller parts, has been extended. The cost of spare parts has remained largely constant in real terms since the early 1990s, although there are periodically supply problems for specific parts from some suppliers. Currency fluctuations, such as those seen during the period after the Brexit referendum in 2016, are a key influence.

Buses have become much more complex, with sophisticated electronics, hybrid and electric drives, GPS, wi-fi and other systems all using power derived from the drive train (engine and gearbox). Maintaining these requires new skills as well as increasing the number of parts that may need maintenance or replacement. The new skills needed for these more sophisticated vehicles present huge challenges in terms of both recruitment and training.

Equipment Costs

These costs cover to the provision of vehicles and the other equipment ("fixed assets") needed to provide a modern bus service. The type of equipment a bus company will require includes:
- The buses themselves and other vehicles
- Ticket machines and back office support systems
- Radios and other vehicle location equipment, plus the back-office support
- Maintenance equipment (ramps, tools, diagnostic computers etc.)
- Administrative equipment such as PCs, printers and other computer hardware.

The charges for these will occur in two forms, depending on the way in which the assets are funded.

This is an important distinction, as it affects how profits are calculated and influences headline measures such as "operating margins" which we shall discuss later. The two methods are:
- **Owned Assets**. These appear on the company's balance sheet and the costs are represented by an annual depreciation charges which appear in the company's accounts. The purchase of these assets may be funded by the company's own cash, by loans or by hire/lease purchase. The cost of interest payments arising from the loan or lease will be accounted for separately, and these sums need to be met from operating profits.
- **Leased Assets**, which are rented (known as "operating leases"). Ownership remains with the leasing company, so the value does not appear on the company's balance sheet. A straightforward periodic rental charge is paid. This reflects the provision for depreciation, the interest costs and a risk premium charged by the lessor.

Claims

Insurance and claim costs have been increasing in recent years, and account for 3% of the overall cost of bus operation. Operators have attempted to control these by anti-fraud measures, use of video recording, improved driver training and monitoring, and by revised risk profiling.

The Primary Drivers of Cost

Historically, bus industry costs were benchmarked and measured as a charge per mile. Changes in average cost per mile were regularly reported, and these numbers were used as the basis for calculating fares and fare increases throughout the 1950s and 1960s.

In the early 1970s, as cost accountancy became a more exact science, it became clear that time rather than distance was the major driver of bus operating costs. This was because labour was the industry's largest cost item: the size of the wage bill was driven by the number of hours worked – a much more important figure than the number of miles run.

Such an approach was particularly useful when it came to splitting costs over different routes, networks or depots.

The number of hours for which operators need to run their buses is mainly a function of speed. This will determine:
- how long the bus will take to run from one terminus to another
- how many revenue-earning trips can be run by each bus in a day
- how many drivers will be required to provide the service.

The average speed at which buses can run will depend on a combination of factors, including:
- the types of road on which it runs (including local topography)
- how congested the roads are
- what parking restrictions there are and how these are enforced
- the number of stops
- how long the bus has to wait at each stop.

The key variables in driving the cost of our bus routes are therefore **time** and **speed**. Some costs, particularly fuel, oil and tyres, will also depend on **distance** – though of course fuel consumption is also influenced to a measurable extent by speed.

Calculating the Resources Needed

Having established what governs the resources needed to run a bus service (time, speed and distance), it is possible to calculate the level of resources, or inputs, that will be required to operate a given route. From there, we can calculate the cost of providing the service.

The figures we need to know are:
- The time taken from one end of the route to the other
- The hours of operation
- The frequency of operation

Worked Example - How Fast?

An urban bus route runs for around 3½ miles (6 km) between the town centre and a local suburb – a round trip of 12 km. The service runs every ten minutes (six departures per hour) between 0600 and 1900 and every 20 minutes from 1900 to midnight.

In relatively uncongested traffic, a network can achieve an average speed of 12 mph (19.3 kph). Narrow roads and frequent stops might mean a fall to 10.3mph (16.5 kph). More serious congestion will drive it down to 9.5 mph (15.2 kph), or even lower.

Worked Example - the Difference that Speed Makes

- At 12 mph, the route will take 37.5 minutes to run a round trip from the town centre and back again, requiring 4 buses.
- At 10.3 mph, the time will rise to 43.7 minutes. The route will now need 5 buses, with one extra needed to cover the extra time and maintain the frequency.
- At 9.5 mph. the time rises to 47.4 minutes, and the uncertainties of traffic congestion lead the operator to increase recovery time to 4 minutes per trip. This means that 6 buses will now be required to run the 10-minute frequency.

Clearly, the slowest journey needs significantly more resources to deliver the same frequency and will therefore be much more expensive to operate. We will discuss these costs and how they work later in the chapter.

Worked Example - Resource Calculations

Looking at the town service we discussed earlier in the chapter, we have established that the route runs every ten minutes from 0600 in the morning until 1900, and then every 20 minutes from 1900 until 2400, seven days a week.

At 11.8 mph:
- Two buses will work for 18 hours day and two will work for 13 hours a day, a total of 62 bus hours a day. If the service runs for 363 days a year, the annual total will be 22,506.
- Paid staff hours, allowing for sickness, holidays, and unexpected absence, would total 29,258.
- Between the buses will cover 1,116 km per day. The annual figure would be 405,000.

At 10.3 mph:
- Two buses will work for 18 hours a day and three for 13. A total of 80 bus hours, amounting to 29,040 per annum (29% more).
- Paid hours would be 37,752 (up 29%).
- The distance run would remain the same.

At 9.5 mph:
- three buses will work for 18 hours a day and three for 13. Bus hours rise to 93 per day, 33,759 per annum (up 50% from base case).
- Paid hours would be 50,639 (also up 50%).
- Again, the distance run would be the same.

These are the key inputs that will enable us to calculate the costs of operation of our route.

- The distance travelled

From this information, we can calculate:
- the number of vehicles we need
- the number of drivers we will need to employ.
- the distance each bus will cover and therefore how much fuel and oil will be needed, and use of tyres.

The hours of operations create the basic timetable that will be used to create schedules for drivers to work. These will include time at the start of the shift to check vehicles, access important information and generally prepare for their shift. Once the bus is out in service, drivers will have to travel to a point at which their duty will begin and that of another driver will finish. At some point in the day, the driver will be entitled to one or more breaks, both to comply with the law and staff agreements, based on what is fair and reasonable in each operating area (taking account of the stress of traffic conditions, etc.). Once those schedules have been constructed, they will typically operate to the same pattern for the 5 work days in each week, with a different schedule for Saturday and Sunday timetables. We then have to allow for sickness and holiday cover. Taking all this into account, the number of staff required

Worked Example - The Cost of Operation

Our model then calculates the expected cost of operating our route at the three different speeds:
- At 11.8mph, the total is £1,067,000 per annum
- At 10.3mph, the costs rise to £1,292,000, an increase of 21%
- At 9.5mph, there is a further increase to £1,516,000, 42% higher than the base.

Worked Example - Target Operating Profit

In order to achieve a 7.5% profit margin, the operator needs to earn 8.1% more than the costs of operation. We can see the effect that the different speeds have on the profit needed:
- At 11.8mph, the figure is £86,000
- At 10.3mph, the target rises to £104,000
- At 9.5mph, there is a further increase to £122,000

Worked Example - Target Revenue and Patronage

Nationally, the average revenue per passenger in 2018/19 was £1.32. Let us assume that our service earns a similar figure.
At the three speeds, the target revenue and patronage would be as follows:
- At 11.8mph, annual target is £1,148,000 from 869,000 passengers
- At 10.3mph, annual target is £1,388,000 from 1,052,000 passengers
- At 9.5mph, annual target is £1,629,000 from 1,234,000 passengers

would be 16 for the fastest speed, 20 for the 10.3mph scenario and 24 for the 9.5 mph case.

How much does it cost?

The annual cost of operating our sample service can be calculated using the data we now have about the resources required and unit cost information taken from the PTIS *Bus Industry Monitor* database.

As discussed in Chapter 3 below, we estimate that the operator needs to make a 7.5% operating profit in order to meet their financial obligations. This figure enables us to estimate what the annual cash profit needs to be and see how it changes with the speed of the service. The increase in profit is needed to fund the extra equipment required to run the service at the slower speeds.

Once we have a target revenue figure, we can also estimate the number of passengers we will need to carry in order to achieve that target.

If we add the profit needed to the costs of operation, we know how much revenue we need to earn from passengers. If we know the typical average fare per passenger, we can also calculate how many passengers we need to carry each year in order to achieve our targets.

We can see from these figures what a crucial difference the speed of operation makes to our ability to run successful, viable bus services. As traffic congestion increases, speeds deteriorate and so more revenue is needed to cover the costs of operation.

At the same time, however, lower speeds make the bus service less attractive, making it more difficult to attract more passengers. If the bus cannot go as quickly, journey times become longer, whilst congestion makes them less predictable. Buses are less able to compete effectively, and therefore passenger numbers are liable to fall rather than increase. We will consider this in more detail in Chapter 7 below.

When this happens, the only way that the bus company can earn the revenue it needs is to put prices up. Even though revenue increases, the number of passengers falls again, so reinforcing a cycle of decline. This is illustrated in Figure 1-2 overleaf.

Figure 1-2: The Bus Industry's Vicious Circle

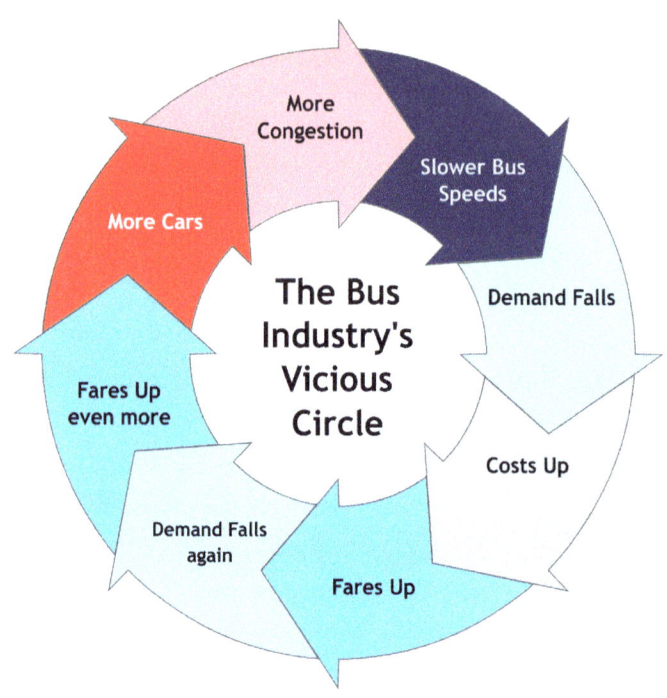

2
Trends in Unit Costs

Labour

Background

Historically, wages and salaries tend to increase at a faster rate than general inflation; the bus industry needs to keep pace in order to attract and retain staff – especially as bus driving inevitably involves shift work and unsocial hours. In addition, the cost of pension provision has risen over recent years (and is expected to rise higher still). Some companies face significant pension deficits which will need to be addressed.

The trends are illustrated in Figure 2-1 below, from which it will be seen that there were continuous rises in real unit labour costs from 1997/98 until the start of the recession in 2007/08. Thereafter there

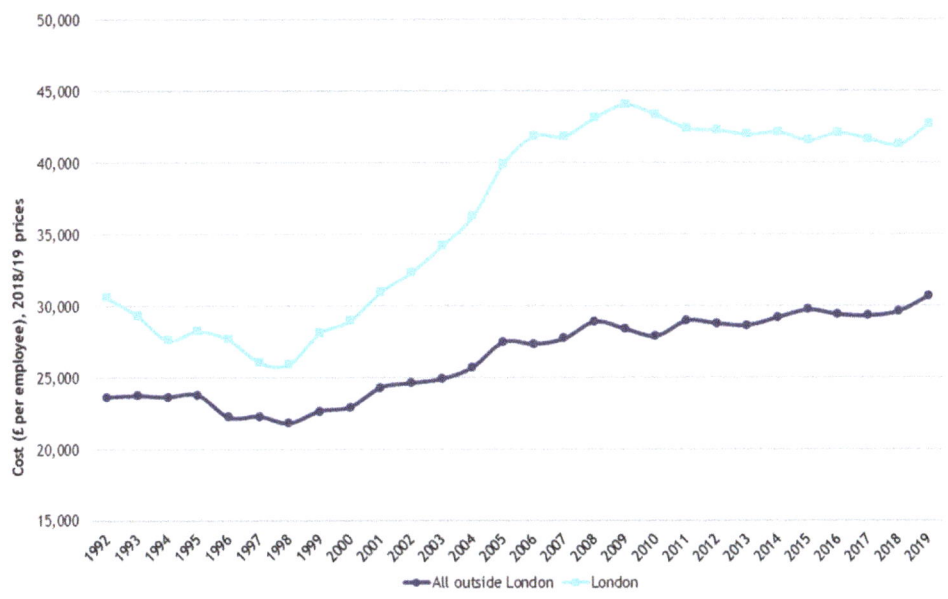

Figure 2-1: Trends in Bus Industry Labour Costs since 1992
Constant (2018/19) Prices

Source: PTIS Bus Industry Monitor database

were several years of real-term falls. However, costs in recent years have started to rise again, largely driven by increases in employer pension contributions.

Productivity

In many other sectors of the economy, it is possible to increase wages without raising prices. This is done by increasing productivity, by reductions in raw materials costs or by increasing sales. However, in the bus industry, the scope for productivity improvements is limited, raw materials costs have tended to rise in recent years and – with some notable exceptions – overall volumes have tended to reduce rather than increase.

It is possible to improve driver and vehicle scheduling or change working practices – but the available gains have in most cases already been achieved during the last 30 years.

One of the key influences on productivity is the speed at which bus services can run. Increasing traffic congestion has tended to result in bus services becoming slower. As we saw in Chapter 1, running more slowly requires more vehicles and more drivers to provide the same level of

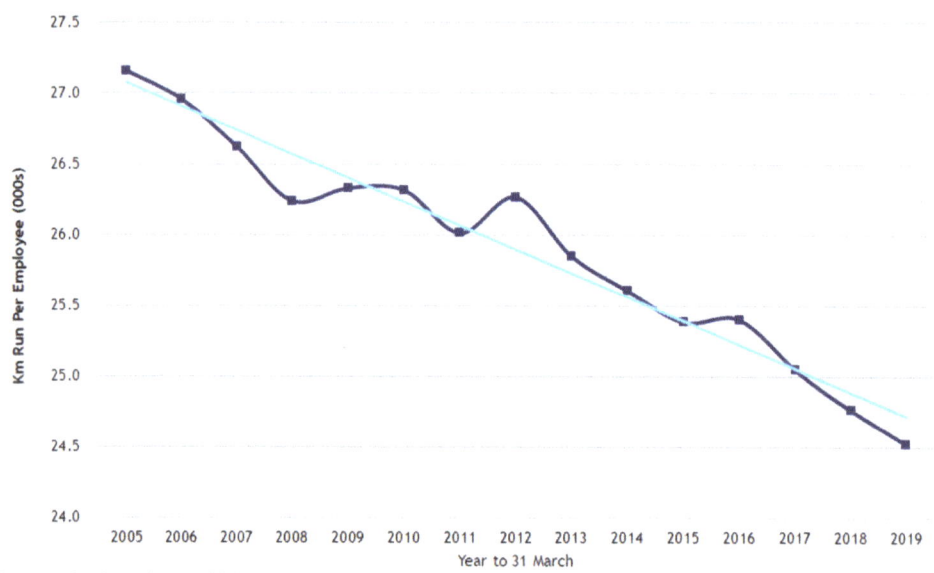

Figure 2-2: Km run per platform staff member since 2005

Source: PTIS analysis of DfT Bus Statistics

service. Modelling work undertaken by the author for the Commission for Integrated Transport and the Department for Transport in 2006 and 2007 suggested that each 1% change in speed affected bus operating costs by 0.8%.

Evidence shows that there has been a fall in vehicle speeds over the last decade. This, coupled with other changes, has reduced industry productivity. DfT provides statistics for staff employed by local bus operators, and an analysis of these suggests that there has been a fall of almost 9% in platform staff productivity since 2005, as seen in Figure 2-2.

Other Costs

Fuel Prices

These are volatile and subject to sudden spikes and troughs, driven in the first decade of the century by:
- political instability in the Middle East
- growth in demand from other parts of the world, notably China

Operators have attempted to mitigate some of the uncertainty in pricing by forward buying stocks of fuel at fixed prices (known as hedging). This reduced short-term volatility, but the new costs have to be faced eventually.

Because of these changes, the overall percentage of costs accounted for by fuel increased from 9% to 17.7% between 2006 and 2014, before gradually falling back to its 2019 level of 12.9%.

Longer term contracts can alleviate the worst impacts of fuel price increases, but the most advantageous terms are likely to be obtained by large groups. Consequently, smaller stand-alone operators are more vulnerable to short-term fuel price increases.

Government policy on fuel taxation is also a major factor. The remission of 100% of fuel duty was first introduced in the 1965 Finance Act, and continued unchanged until the 1993 budget, when the Government decided to freeze the value of the rebate for the 1992-1997 Parliament, at a time when the fuel tax escalator was in operation. This position was initially maintained by the incoming Blair Government.

In 1998, though, the rebate was fixed at 80% of duty, a position that remained unaltered for a decade. The rebate was renamed Bus Service

Operators' Grant (BSOG) under the Transport Act 2000, and reform of the way it is calculated and paid was considered on several occasions in the 1990s but rejected. A further review of the grant in England was promised by the Government in its new National Bus Strategy published in March 2021. Given the accelerating move towards low-carbon vehicles, a scheme that links payment to miles run by diesel-powered buses is seen as no longer appropriate.

Powers over BSOG were devolved in Wales and Scotland, where the link with fuel duty has since been formally broken:
- in Scotland, a fixed payment per mile operated has been instituted.
- in Wales the funding for BSOG has been combined with other transport grants into Bus Services Support Grant (BSSG), and total spending cut by more than 25%. From April 2013, the scheme was devolved to the local transport partnerships.

In England, DfT uses the rebate mechanism to encourage the use of

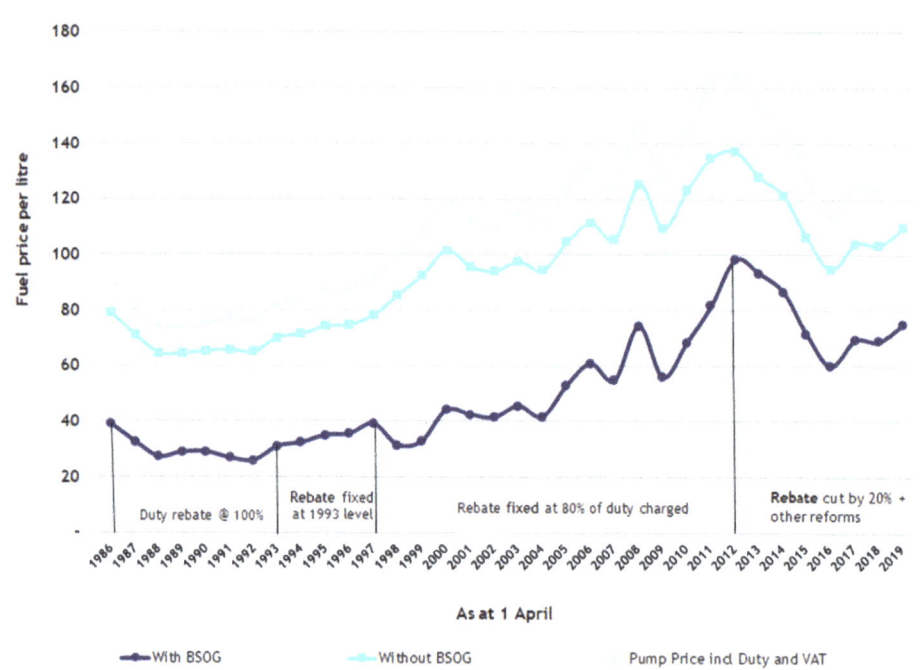

Figure 2-3: Bus Industry Diesel Fuel Prices since 1986
Constant (2019) prices

Source: PTIS Analysis. Figures on fuel prices from Transport Statistics Great Britain

'greener' buses and fuels and other 'desirable' policy outcomes such as smartcard availability, or contactless payments. Several steps have been taken. So BSOG was:
- cut by 20% from April 2012.
- devolved to TfL in London from October 2013
- devolved to local authorities from April 2014 for tendered services.
- Reduced to 75% of the national rate in certain designated areas (known as "Better Bus Areas") with the balance devolved to local authorities, also from April 2014.

The latter was agreed in return for submissions by authorities and operators of specific joint plans to improve service delivery.

Because of all these changes, the price paid by bus operators for their fuel doubled in real terms between the turn of the century and 2012. It has fallen back since that peak, though the price of oil remains volatile and consequently fuel costs are a major area of risk for bus operators.

Both Government and the industry are targeting improvements in fuel efficiency: using less fuel will cut costs and reduce the environmental impact of bus services. Alongside work on alternative propulsion methods, this is beginning to address a long-term problem whereby buses have tended to become less fuel efficient – primarily because they have become heavier. There are several reasons for this:
- Regulatory, including noise and emission reductions
- Customer expectations, for improved seating, wheelchair ramps, bigger windows and better ventilation
- Manufacturing, where there is now a tendency to use heavier HGV components in volume bus production. This keeps the initial capital costs lower than they would be if these components had to be specifically designed and manufactured for buses.
- The growth in traffic congestion means that buses use more fuel as they need to start and stop more often.

Overheads (including Administration)

Immediately after privatisation, there were huge reductions in overheads, with central works facilities closed, bus depots and bus station sites sold off and layers of management and administrative staff removed.

However, these were "one off" gains, and recent trends have seen

costs start to rise again. This has resulted from:
- the need for additional supervision to improve standards
- rising utility costs
- increased regulation of waste disposal
- staff salaries
- rising rents, property costs, land values and business rates.

Vehicles

Depreciation charges mirror the cost of new buses and other equipment. The cost of new buses has increased in real terms over several years, though this has been accompanied by an improvement in quality.

Bus replacements are rarely if ever 'like for like': newer, more sophisticated models will inevitably be more expensive than their predecessors. In the past, this has been offset by buying smaller vehicles as demand fell; however, the introduction of new low-floor designs from the mid-1990s onwards meant a fall in the number of seats per bus. This meant vehicles had to become larger again in order to accommodate the same number of people.

The introduction of new buses has major benefits for the community, in the form of better accessibility for people with mobility handicaps, better passenger facilities such as charging points and wi-fi and reduced emissions.

In recent years, a major factor in pricing new vehicles has been the value of sterling, which has affected the price of components and indeed complete vehicles if purchased from overseas.

The introduction of low-carbon vehicles, such as battery-electric or hydrogen-fuelled is driving the cost of new vehicles upwards significantly. The price premium tends to be between 50% and 100% compared with a conventional diesel bus - though this may come down in time. In addition, there are infrastructure costs at depots as well - installation of electric charging points or new gas storage facilities. Government funding has in the past plugged up to 90% of the gap, though this is now being reduced to 75%.

Other on-board equipment

The range and complexity of other equipment needed to run a service has also grown in recent years, with a consequent increase in costs.

The humble mechanically-driven ticket machine of the early post war years has been replaced by growingly sophisticated electronic devices, which are themselves significantly more expensive, but also require complex back-office systems.

Active management of the service out on the road has become increasingly important. Radios to maintain contact with drivers out on the road became widespread in urban areas from the 1970s onwards. These are now supplemented by satellite-based automatic vehicle location systems – again requiring more complex back-office systems.

Maintenance Equipment

Vehicle maintenance has also become more sophisticated, with the humble spanner increasingly unable to cope with electric drives and fuel cells, electronic engine-management systems and the need for computerised diagnostic equipment

Summary

The costs of operation inevitably impact on the level of fares which operators seek to charge. As we have seen, bus operating costs tend to rise more quickly than general inflation. The increases result from:
- Increased labour costs
  - Drivers' wages have risen to ensure that the industry is able to recruit enough staff to maintain reliable services
  - Bus driving is generally no longer a 'job of last resort' as wages have increased, with improved quality as a result
  - Increases in the cost of pension provision and social security payments
- Changes in fuel costs
  - changes are periodic and steep, not a continuous process – and sharp increases can be followed by sharp falls.
- Increased cost of new vehicles and other vital equipment
- Reduced productivity, resulting from growing traffic congestion and increased regulation

Increases in cost have generally (but not always) been accompanied by improvements in quality in terms of drivers and vehicles.

3
Bus Industry Profits

Introduction

Whether bus services are run on a commercial model (as in Great Britain outside London), or under a tendered or publicly owned regime, operators still need to earn more in revenue from passengers and/or public authorities than they pay in operating costs (known as an **operating profit**). This is because they need to fund previous borrowing and to invest in new and replacement assets to continue to develop the business.

This chapter discusses these matters in more detail and provides worked examples of how things are calculated.

Raising capital - the creation of obligations

Any new or existing bus company needs to provide physical assets in order to function – buses, depots, workshops, tools, ticketing machines, computers.

It is rare that a company – especially a new one – will have the cash to buy these things outright. Typically, therefore, they borrow the money. This is known as **the capital employed**.

Depending on the type of enterprise, the money may be borrowed from shareholders, from banks and hire purchase companies or from the money markets through government.

In each case, though, borrowing money creates obligations that must be met – that is the law. A company which fails to meet its obligations will go bankrupt. These obligations are:
- to repay loans as they fall due.
- to pay interest on the money borrowed
  - to banks and other lenders
  - to shareholders in the form of dividends

The interest and the dividends paid are together known as **the cost of capital**.

The major difference between loans and shares is, of course, that interest *must* be paid on loans to avoid a default situation, whereas shareholders only receive a dividend if the company has been successful and can afford to pay one. There are strict rules in company law governing when and if a dividend can be paid.

In simple terms, in order to stay in business, an operator must earn enough **operating profit** to cover its **cost of capital**.

How much profit?

The Theory

Given the information we have just discussed – the capital employed and the cost of capital, we can calculate the level of operating profit that an operator needs to make in order to stay in business and develop for the future. Given our knowledge of how much it costs to operate our bus networks, we can then calculate how much revenue is needed.

In other industries, economic regulators have been making such calculations for some 30 years, since the first privatisation of utility companies created the need for such regulation in the mid-1980s.

Over the years since 2010, therefore, PTIS has tried to show how a target return on capital employed can be calculated, and then show how this translates into a target operating profit margin – which is the most widely understood and easy to calculate measurement of performance.

The Model

A brief explanation follows, but a fuller version can be found in our regular annual ***Bus Industry Performance*** reports, which provides updates of the figures as the market changes. The commentary below relates to our 2020 analysis, based on the 2018/19 financial year.

Our model on profit asks four key questions:
- What assets does the company require to provide its service?
- What level of return should be allowed on those assets?
- How much will the business cost to run?
- What funds will the company need to borrow and how much will it cost?

Armed with those four pieces of data, it is then possible to determine:

Figure 3-1: The Need for Profits in the Bus Industry

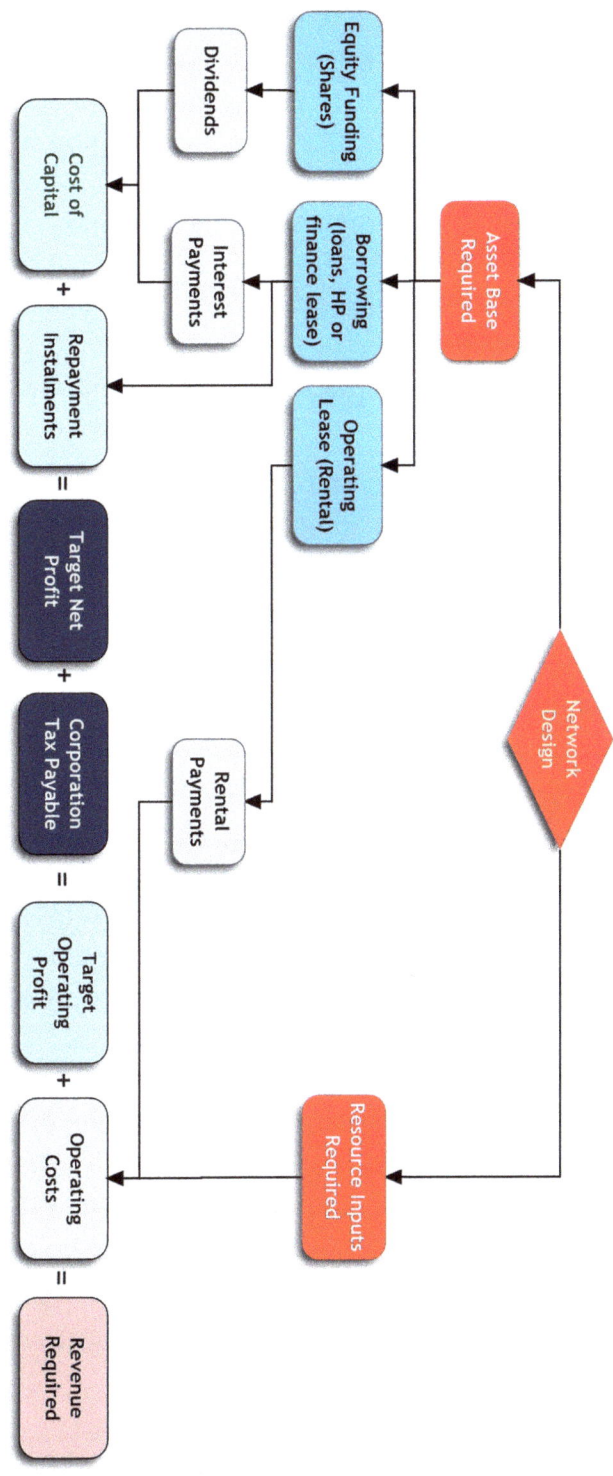

- what the profits should be
- how much revenue the company needs in order to meet these obligations and targets, given its level of operating costs.

The methodology is illustrated in graphic form at Figure 3-1 above.

It is important to note that this analysis and approach holds good *whatever the regulatory regime in force*. Thus, the decisions on service levels and network design that determine the *Asset Base Required* can be made by a commercial operator or by a tendering authority such as Transport for London. The *Revenue Required* can come in the form of individual fares paid by passengers, concessionary fares reimbursement and other grants, or as "cost plus" payments by tendering authorities, as in London.

It is misleading to suggest, as some have done in the past, that bus services would be cheaper to operate under a quality contract or 'franchised' regime because the operator would not need to make as much profit.

How it Works

Using data from our *Bus Industry Monitor* database and the PTIS Bus Operating Model, plus expert advice, we have constructed the finances of three typical bus companies.

Note that capital employed is lower in London. This is because operators there tend to use operating leases (effectively a form of contract hire) for their vehicles in order to tie the cost and age of the vehicles more closely to the life of TfL contracts. Since the value of such assets is not carried on the company's balance sheet, this decision reduces the capital employed. It also pushes interest charges down. At the same time, though, it increases operating costs because the operator is obliged to pay rental charges to the leasing company that owns the assets.

The operating costs in London are double that of the shire operator, because:
- the operating day is much longer, requiring more staff
- speeds are slower, increasing the number of drivers needed and the fuel used
- unit labour costs in the capital are much higher.

Worked Example - The Scenario

Take three bus companies each with a fleet of 200 buses running from three depots. One runs in an English Shire area, one in a major conurbation and one in London. The fleets contain a mix of vehicles suitable for their market, with an average age of eight years. In London, the fleet is younger and more expensive to meet TfL requirements.

The value of the required assets has been calculated, giving us the net debt, shareholder funds and capital employed for each business. These are illustrated in Figure 3-2 below.

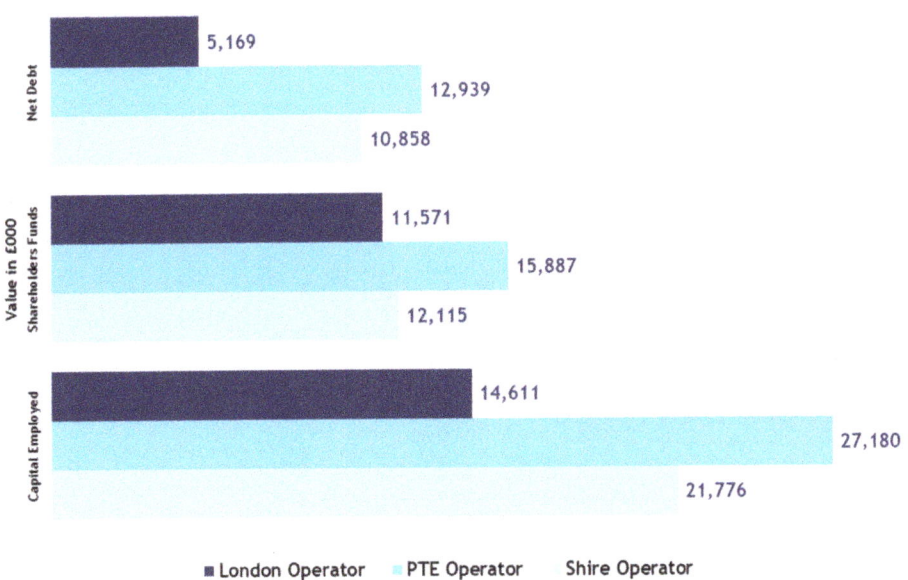

Figure 3-2: Worked Example - Key Balance Sheet Figures

Worked Example - The Targets

The revenue and profit targets that each company would set itself are based on:
- The cost of borrowing (currently around 6% real)
- The target for dividend payments (3.85% on shareholder funds*)
- The need for replacement capital expenditure

Adding these three together gives the target net profit, as illustrated in Figure 3-3 below. Add the tax payable to give the pre-tax profit. Then add the costs of operation to give the amount of revenue each company needs to earn from passengers or the tendering authority.

* - Based on current dividend yields for FTSE250 companies, December 2019.

Figure 3-3: Worked Example - Key Target Figures

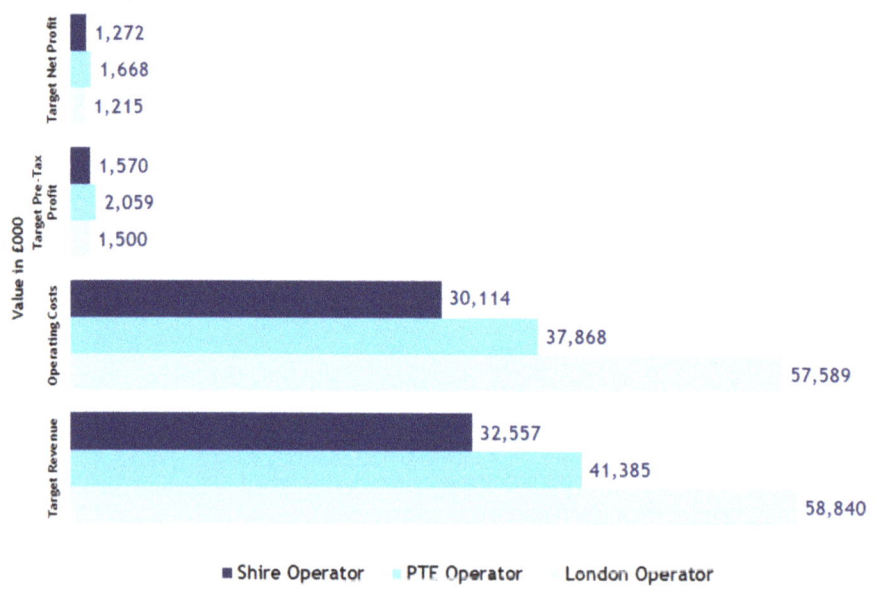

Worked Example - Margins and Returns

If the target revenue is achieved in each case, we can see how that would translate into comparative measures of profit margins and returns. This is illustrated in Figure 3-4 below.

For companies outside London, the model suggests that operating profit margins need to be between 7.5% and 8.0% in order to allow operators to cover their cost of capital.

This shows how the different business model in London means that lower returns are needed, and the target cash profit translates into a much lower margin.

Figure 3-4: Worked Example - Margins and Returns

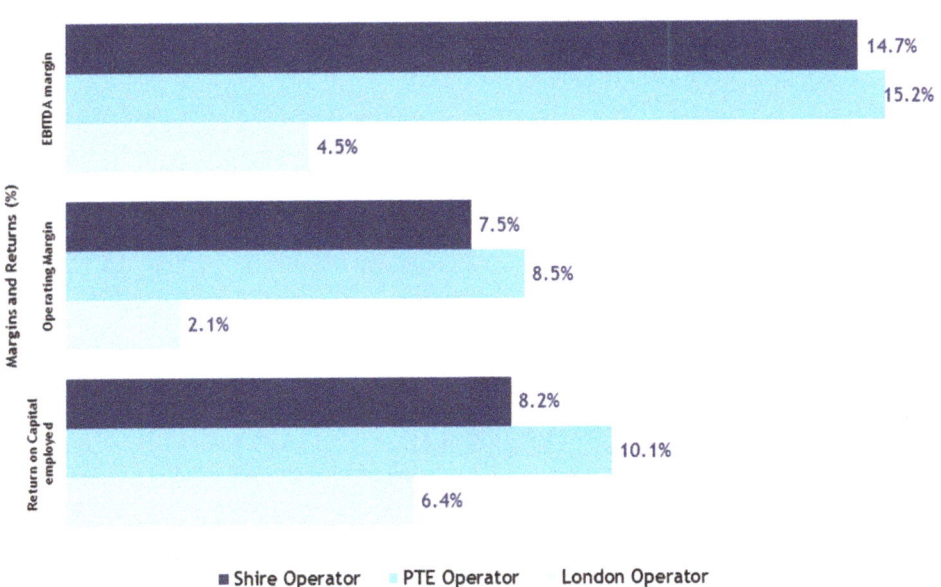

Worked Example – What Happens to the Profit

First call on the operating profit is to meet the company's obligations. These are to:

- pay Corporation Tax
- pay interest on the company's borrowing
- pay any instalments due on the borrowing

Next comes the need to fund investment in new products or business expansion, and if possible, a transfer to reserves to help the company survive in any bad times. Only then can dividends be paid to shareholders to reward them for their ownership and risk.

The way this would work for our three sample companies is illustrated in Figure 3-5 below.

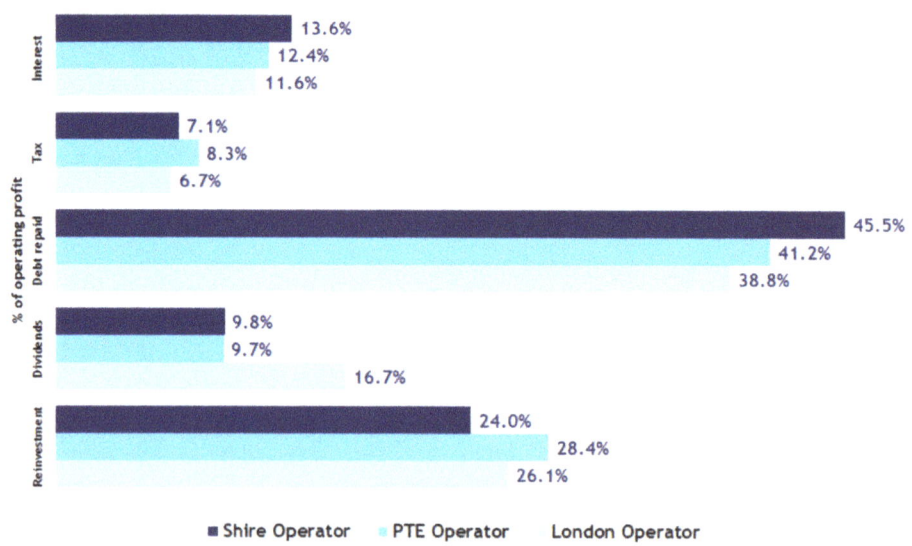

Figure 3-5: Breakdown of Operating Profit Distribution (%)

Profits earned

In the days before the onset of the recession, when interest rates and dividend yields were much higher, the quoted groups set target of around 15% for their subsidiaries to earn as an EBIT margin. As inflation has fallen and interest rates have been at record lows, the cost of capital has fallen, so driving the required profit margins downwards. Thus, as we have seen, a target of around 8% should enable most companies to provide an acceptable return on capital and meet their financial obligations.

However, in practice, few companies have ever achieved these levels, and profit levels across the industry remain at slightly below the required level.

At best, the industry 12% to 13% between 1998 and 2000. Since that time, profitability generally has declined, especially since 2015, as shown in Figure 3-6.

Figure 3-6: Bus Industry EBIT Margins
Companies outside London since 1991/92

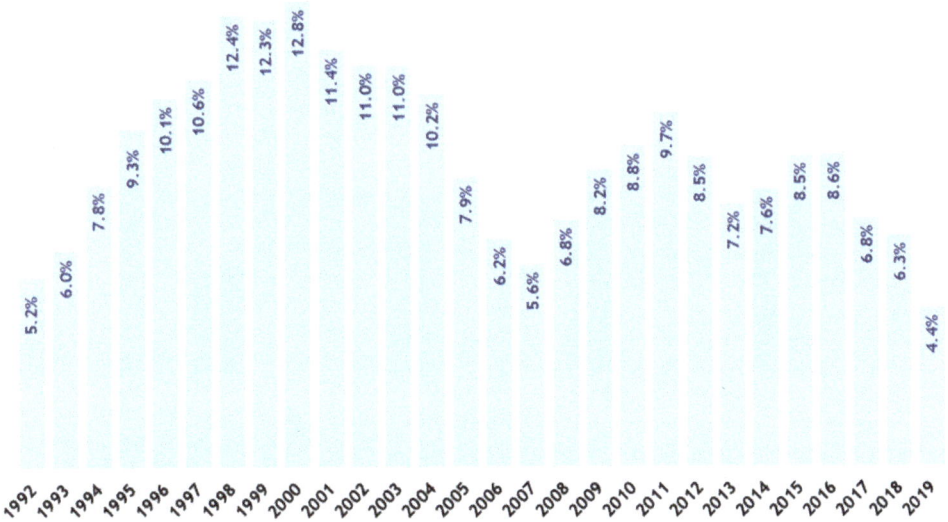

Source: PTIS Bus Industry Monitor database

In addition to wide variations by individual companies there are significant regional variations in bus company profits, and these are shown in Figure 3-7 for the most recent three years, running up to 2018/19. Bus company profits in 2018/19 were highest in the metropolitan counties, but as can be seen have fallen in all areas, though there was some recovery in Wales in the most recent year.

It will be appreciated that, in the case of the London companies, turnover represents payments from Transport for London, and not fares revenue.

Overall Conclusions

The worked example suggests that operating profit (EBIT) margins need to be in the range 7.5% to 8.0% in order to enable bus companies to meet their financial obligations and to invest in the future.

As can be seen from the graph at Figure 3-7, current average profit

Figure 3-7: Bus Industry EBIT Margins by Area
Three years to 2018/19

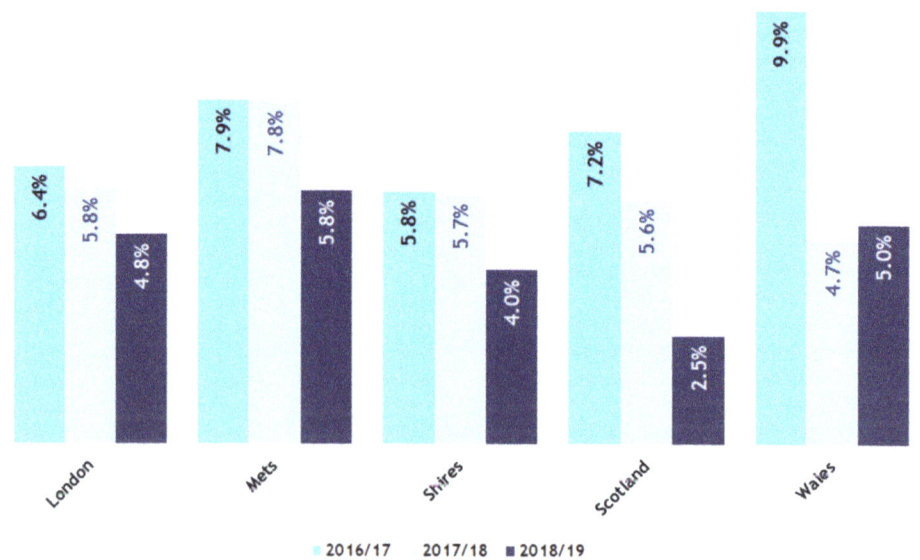

Source: PTIS Bus Industry Monitor database

margins across the country are some way short of this level, at between 5.8% and 2.5%.

There is a direct link between these targets and the level of interest rates in the economy. At the time of writing, interest rates are at historic lows, and therefore so is the cost of capital: the interest on borrowing and the level of returns expected by shareholders. Once these costs start to rise again, so will the level of profits needed to fund them.

Our modelling work suggests that profit margins need to rise by 0.8% for each 1% increase in interest rates. Any rise in inflation during the post-Covid era would clearly affect this as well.

In London, the analysis suggests that the differences in cost structure and business model mean that operators need an operating margin of around 2-3% in order to achieve the same return on capital. This will vary depending on the funding mechanism chosen by the operator for their fleet, and the consequent mix between owned and leased vehicles. The analysis of the most recent accounts suggests that, broadly, the necessary returns are being achieved.

Figure 4-1: The Marketing Mix for Bus Services

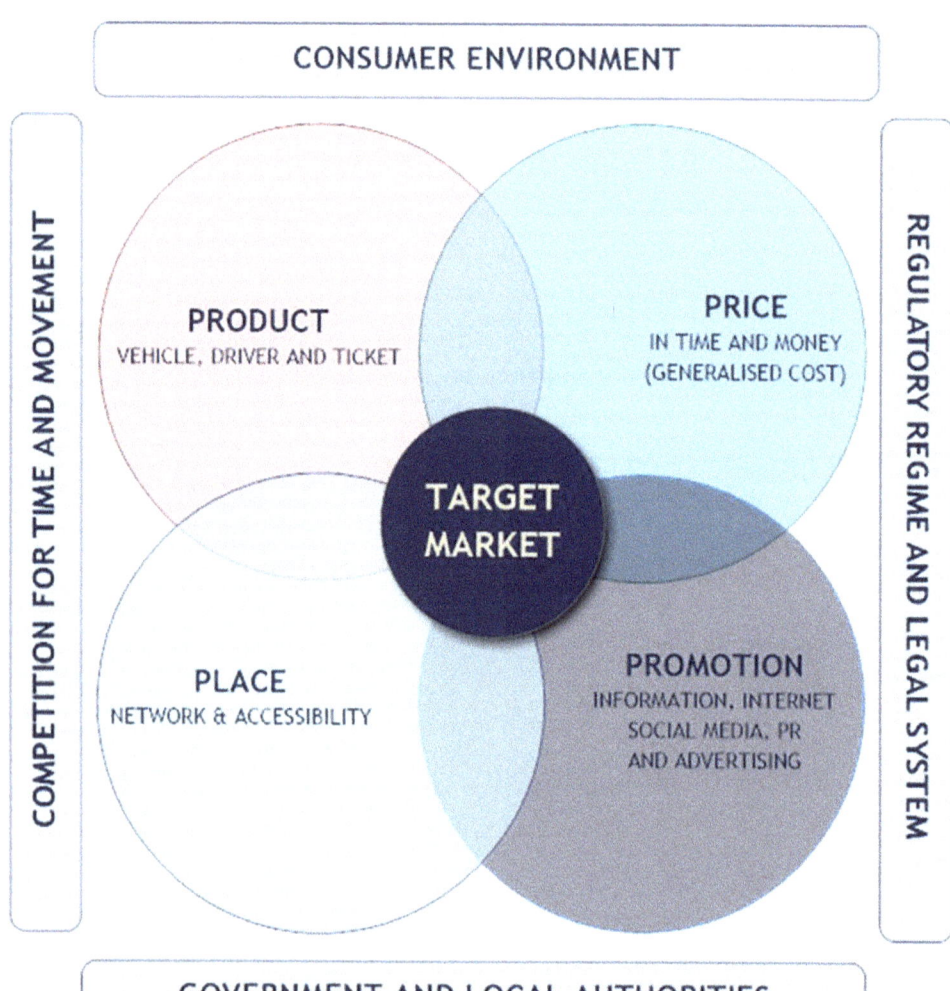

4
Demand for Bus Services

What drives demand?

The important point to remember about all forms of transport is that demand is *derived* from people's need or desire to do other things. This can be as mundane as going to work or school every day, the occasional need to visit a hospital or a bank or more exciting things like going to the cinema or to meet friends in a bar.

After deciding whether to go out, consumers then make a *mode choice*. For instance, they can walk to the shops, cycle to school or drive the car to work. Or they can use public transport, like a bus, train or tram.

Thus, the number of journeys people take by bus will be derived from people's need to access services and the mode choice they make about how to get to they want to go.

One way to think about this is to use a traditional "marketing mix" diagram, still widely used in the marketing of more conventional goods and services. We have adapted this for bus services, and it is shown in Figure 4-1 opposite.

This relates the traditional "four Ps" of marketing analysis – Place, Product, Price and Promotion – to different aspects of bus operation.

Almost equally important, though, are the four outer rectangles, because these set the context in which the industry must work – government policy at national and local levels, the consumer environment (in simple terms, whether buses are "cool" or not), competition from other modes and industry regulation.

This approach is fine, and it is a useful way to understand the task that the industry faces in winning passengers. However, it does not help us to quantify the demand and to understand how it is made up. A complex web of factors is involved, including the size and make-up of the local population, economic prosperity, car ownership and the attributes of the product itself – frequency, speed, reliability and price.

Figure 4-2: Factors influencing the Demand for Bus Services

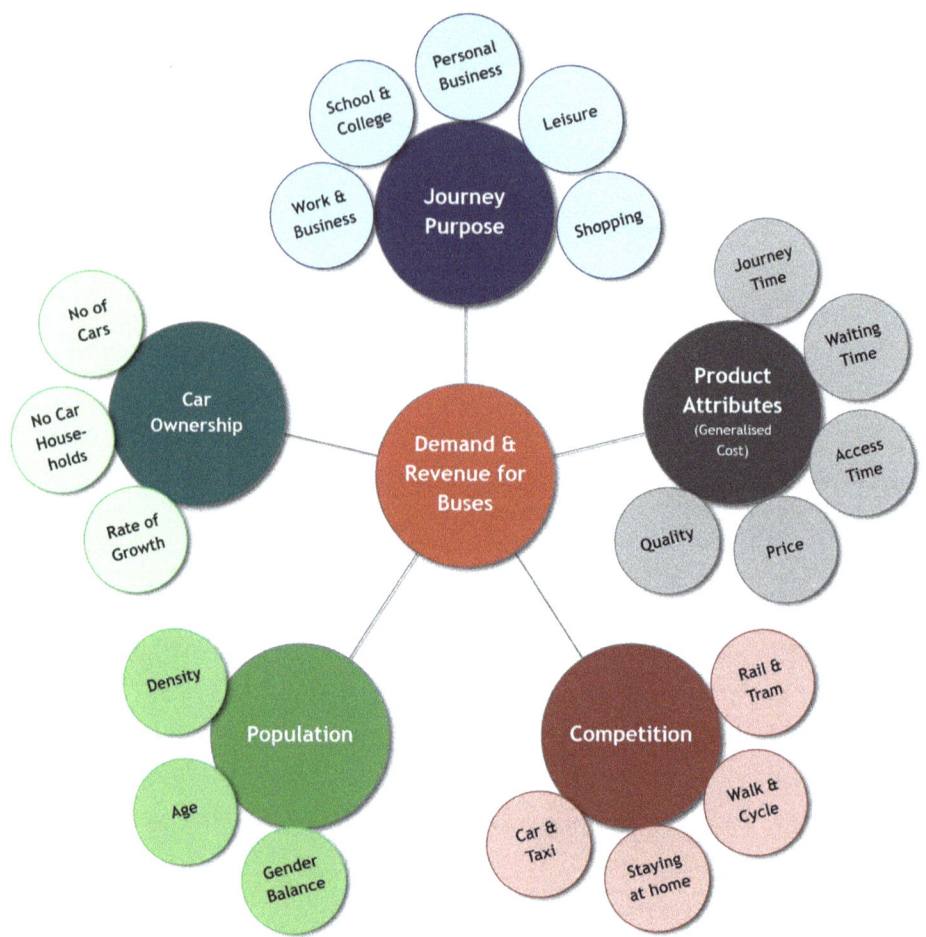

These all mix together to determine how much demand there is, and whether it goes up or down. A diagram of this mixture of factors can be seen at below.

Each of the main subjects is considered in more detail in the chapters which follow this one. In brief, the principal social changes that have influenced bus demand since 1950 may be summarised as:
- The growth in the ownership and use of the private car
- The spread of television and the decline in attendance at cinemas and other live entertainment
- Major changes in shopping habits. This is a continuing process of evolution, but has happened in three broad phases:

- the growth in the use of refrigerators and freezers and the growth of supermarket shopping in the late 1950s and early 1960s.
- the growth of out of town/edge of town supermarkets and hypermarkets more accessible by car and less by bus in the 1980s and 1990s
- the growth of online shopping and reduction of visits to the High Street – an ongoing trend.

• Shifts in the labour market with the decline in traditional industries such as mining and manufacturing, and more diverse distribution of jobs as major manufacturing plants have shed labour or closed.

One thing stands out from this analysis: how few of these factors are within the control of the bus operators themselves. Even amongst the product attributes, key aspects are much more heavily influenced by others, such as local councils and highway authorities.

Overall Volumes of Travel

The chart at Figure 4-3 shows how overall demand for travel in the UK has grown since the early 1950s. In total, we travel around four

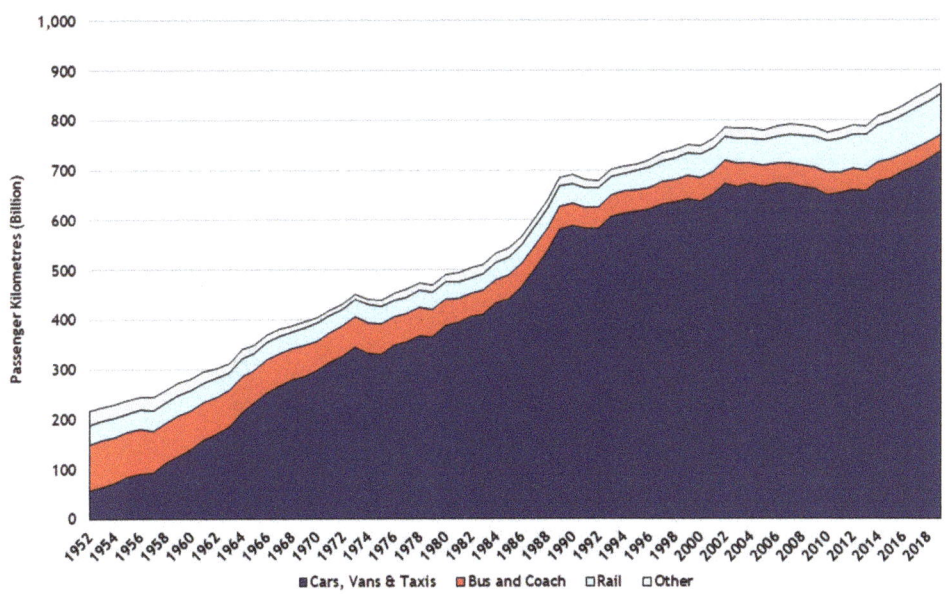

Figure 4-3: Overall Demand for Travel by Mode since 1952

Source: PTIS analysis of Transport Statistics Great Britain, DfT

times as many passenger kilometres as we did in 1952, and most of those journeys (84.5% at the last count) are by private vehicle.

As we can see from Figure 4-4, the market share of the different modes has changed massively from those early post-war years, when only 27% of journeys were by car, whilst 42% were by bus and another 17% by train. The comparison between the 1952 and 2016 figures for the market share of each mode, reinforce the point.

As a result of these changes, the volume of passengers travelling by bus has been in long term decline for over six decades.

Demand for local bus services in Great Britain halved between 1950 and the early 1970s, and virtually halved again by the mid-1990s (see Figure 4-5 below). The numbers reached a low point of 4.3 billion in the late 1990s, before staging a recovery, led by the introduction of free concessionary travel in England outside London, and by strong growth in the capital.

However, growing congestion, the development of internet shopping and cuts in service provision mean that numbers are now falling again, even in the capital. The chart at Figure 4-6 illustrates the split between London and the rest of Great Britain at five-yearly intervals since 1950.

Figure 4-4: Market Share by Mode, 1952 and 2016

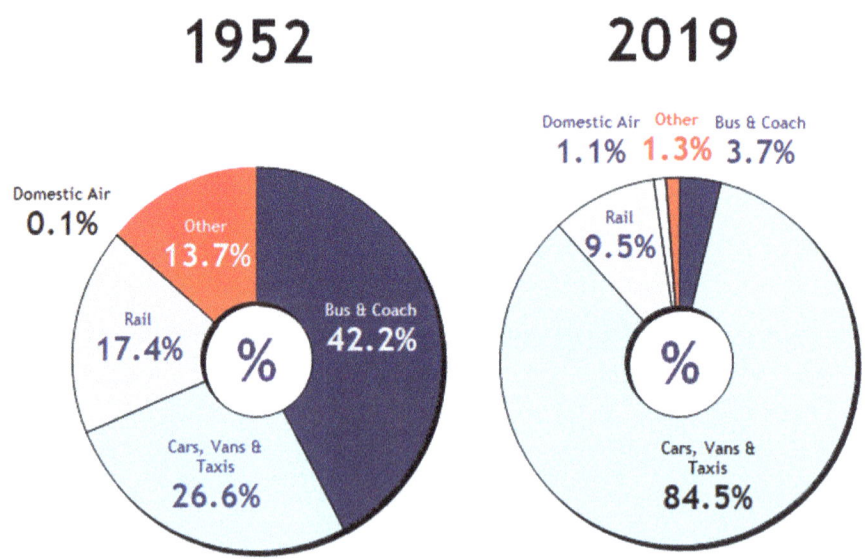

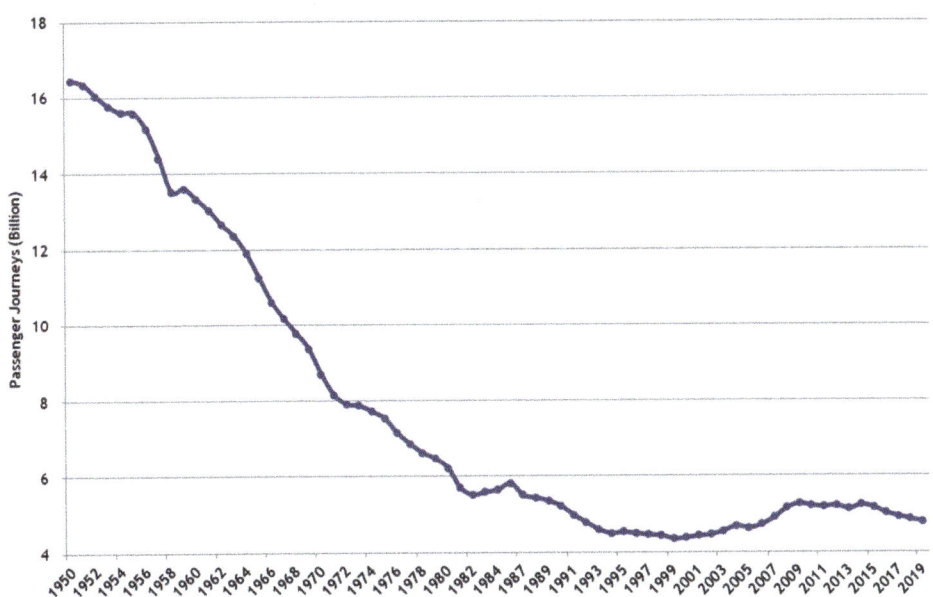

Figure 4-5: Bus Demand since 1950

Source: Department for Transport Annual Bus Statistics. Figures include trams and trolleybuses between 1950 and 1972

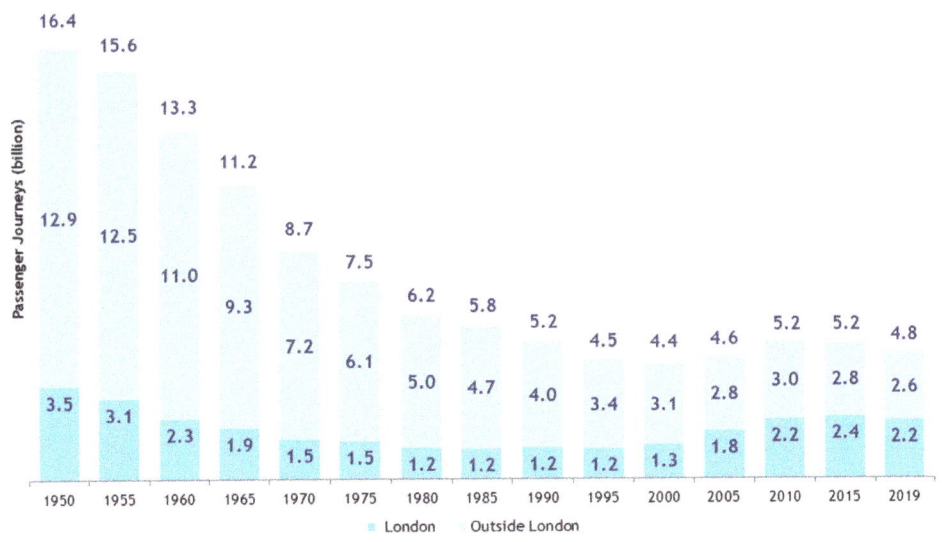

Figure 4-6: Bus Patronage inside and outside London

Source: Department for Transport Annual Bus Statistics. Pre-1970 London statistics from Barker & Robbins: A History of London Transport, volume 2, 1900-1974. London figures include trams (1950) and trolleybuses (1950, 1955, 1960). The figures in the two graphs may not necessarily sum because of rounding.

Why Volume Matters

Bus operators have reacted to the decline in demand over the last 50 years in two ways:
- Reducing the volume of services
- Increasing the fares charged

The volume of services has indeed been reduced, though at a much slower rate than demand. Demand for services in terms of passenger kilometres has reduced by 62% since 1960, but the number of kilometres run has only fallen by 23%.

Inevitably, if supply is not reduced, then fares have to rise. This is because the cost of running the remaining services has had to be spread amongst fewer passengers. The worked example illustrates this point.

The combination of rising operating costs and falling passenger volumes seen in the worked example has at times led the industry into a "double bind" of ever-increasing cost per passenger: this has been one of the biggest drivers of fares increases over the years.

Worked Example: Break Even Load

The falls in bus patronage since the 1950s mean that the average number of passengers on each bus has fallen.
- In 1955, the load was 26.6
- By 1970 it had fallen to 18.1
- In 2019, the figure stood at 11.7.

The figures from our sample bus companies suggest that bus operations currently cost around £40.50 per hour.

So, we can see how much each passenger would have to pay in order to cover the cost of an hour's operation.
- If the load is 26.6, the sum needed is £1.52 each
- Once the load has fallen to 18.1, this rises to £2.23
- At the current figure of 11.8, it now stands at £3.45.

If next year the same departure costs 5% more to provide, then the cost per passenger rises to £2.95. But if, at the same time, the average load on the bus falls by 5%, then the cost per passenger rises even further. Therefore, the operator needs 10.5% more revenue from each of the remaining passengers just to maintain his income.

5
Population

Introduction

As we saw in the diagram at Figure 4-2, there are several important variations in the demographic profile of different areas of the country which vitally affect bus demand.

In summary, these are:
- The total number of people in each area (population density)
- The age of those people
- The gender of those people
- Their income
- Whether they have access to cars or not

Each of these is discussed in more detail in the sections below.

Population Density

Why Density is Important

Population density will have a significant effect on the market potential of a local bus network. The more people who live within a given area, the more bus trips that area will be likely to generate.

We can show this in another worked example, illustrated in the graph Figure 5-1 overleaf. In this case, we have taken a given area and looked at how different population densities will affect total bus demand in the area.

In this example, we have taken an area the size of a city such as Bristol or Liverpool at around 110 km². We have then assumed that each person in the area makes around 115 bus trips per year, which is the average for a range of English urban areas. The differences are clear: the area with the population density of 10,000, like Inner London, would generate **13 times** more bus journeys at given trip rates than an area with a population density of around 800 per square kilometre such as South Yorkshire.

It follows from this that more densely populated areas can support a

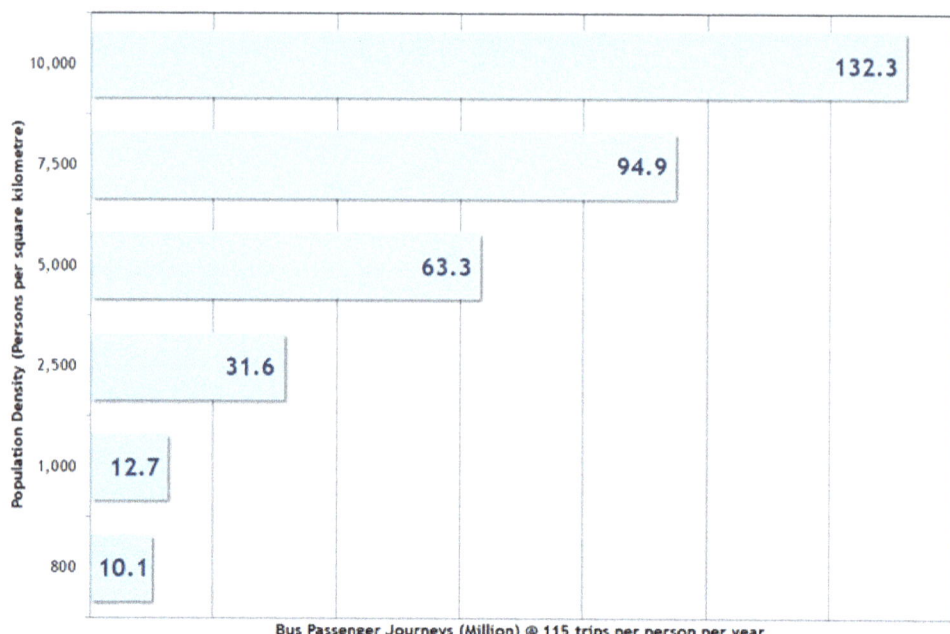

Figure 5-1: Bus Patronage at Different Population Densities

much more intensive bus network, since the demand for trips generated will be much greater, even if trip rates do not vary.

Population Density in England

The 2019 Mid-Year Population Estimates published by the Office for National Statistics Census showed that population density in England is 432 persons per square kilometre.

However, there are huge variations between the most densely and sparsest populated areas. The London Borough of Tower Hamlets was is the most densely populated, accommodating 16,237 persons per square kilometre in 2015. At the other end of the scale, Eden in Cumbria has a density of just 25.

The only areas of the UK with population densities of more than 10,000 are nine Inner London boroughs. Indeed, only two areas outside London even have a population density at more than 5,000 – the cities of Portsmouth and Southampton.

This is another vivid illustration of the way in which London is very different from other urban areas in the UK. Consequently, great care must be taken in thinking that lessons from London about bus demand can be applied elsewhere.

Perhaps surprisingly, other urban areas in the country are much less densely populated. There are only 20 or so local authority areas outside London with densities above 3,500 persons per square kilometre. Perhaps surprisingly, the list excludes:
- the major conurbations of West and South Yorkshire
- the districts of Greater Manchester outside the city of Manchester
- Merseyside (outside the city of Liverpool)
- Tyne and Wear
- Four of the seven West Midland districts

Age and Gender

The Department for Transport's annual National Travel Survey (NTS) gives some perspective on who uses bus services and how frequently. This shows how a person's age and gender affects their use of transport, including buses.

These figures are illustrated graphically in Figure 5-2 below. Across the age range, women make more trips than men. In terms of age, the

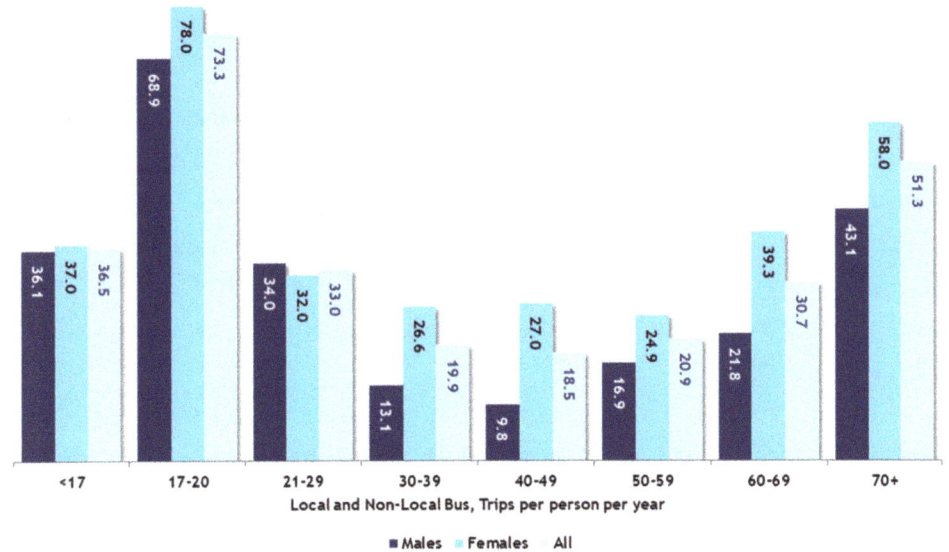

Figure 5-2: Bus Trip Rates by Age and Gender, England 2019

Source: National Travel Survey 2019, DfT

Figure 5-3: Bus Passenger Journeys – breakdown by age
England 2019

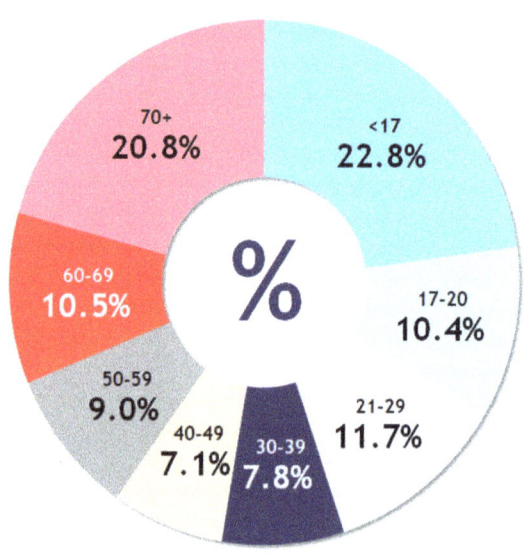

Source: PTIS analysis of National Travel Survey 2019, DfT and 2019 ONS Mid-Year Population Estimates

largest volume of trips by far is made by the 17-20 age group, both male and female. The next most important group are the over 70s, followed by those aged between 60 and 69. Those aged between 40 and 49 make the lowest number of trips.

If we apply these trip rates to the proportions of the population represented by each age group, it is possible to see what proportion of bus use is represented by each group. This is done in the graph at Figure 5-3.

As can be seen, bus travel is predominantly a young person's mode: almost 53% of all trips are taken by the under 40s, and 45% by those under 30. The analysis shows that people aged 60 and above account for 31% of all trips.

Shifts in the age distribution of the population will therefore affect overall volumes of demand, both in specific local areas and across the country as a whole. Notable trends expected to have an impact over the next decade are increases in the number of elderly people and a short-term fall in the number of younger people, which will be reversed in the early 2020s as the effects of an increased birth rate work through.

Socio-Economic Groups

Figure 5-4 shows the percentage of bus use by income groups. People in the group with the lowest 20% of income make the largest proportion of bus journeys, with 31% of all bus journeys measured by trips per person per year. This is closely followed by the second level, but with successive reductions by each income level following.

Nevertheless, 24% of bus trips are made by people in the top two income brackets, who are very likely to have a car available for their trip.

New analysis from the Department for Transport allows us to produce a similar analysis for bus use outside the capital, where it has been suspected for some time that the socio-economic breakdown of bus passengers would be different. This has indeed proved to be the case, with the upper income levels providing a much lower proportion of passengers. This is also contained in Figure 5-4.

Whereas in the country as a whole, the top income group accounts for 19.5% of bus patronage, the same figure outside London is much lower at 9.5%. People in the second highest income group also account

Figure 5-4: Bus Use by income Quintile
England 2019

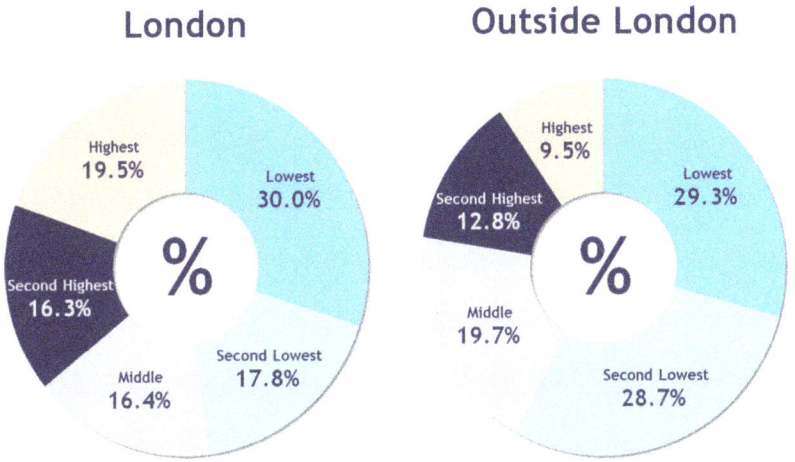

Source: PTIS Analysis of National Travel Survey 2019, DfT and ONS 2019 Mid-Year Population Estimates

for a lower proportion of trips, with correspondingly higher proportions accounted for by people in the middle and second lowest income groups.

Access to Cars

The frequency of bus use remains heavily dependent on access to a car, with bus use in a household falling sharply when a car is acquired. Figure 5-5 below shows the number of trips for persons in a household depending on car ownership and whether they are the main driver or not. The figures are again taken from the Department for Transport's National Travel Survey.

As can be seen, members of households without a car make 84 trips per person per year, but this falls sharply - even amongst non-drivers - once a household acquires a car.

In view of this, it is interesting to reflect on the way car ownership has changed since the mid-1980s. The result, in terms of car ownership per 1,000 people, can be seen in Figure 5-6 below. Growth has been very

Figure 5-5: Bus trips per person per year by car ownership

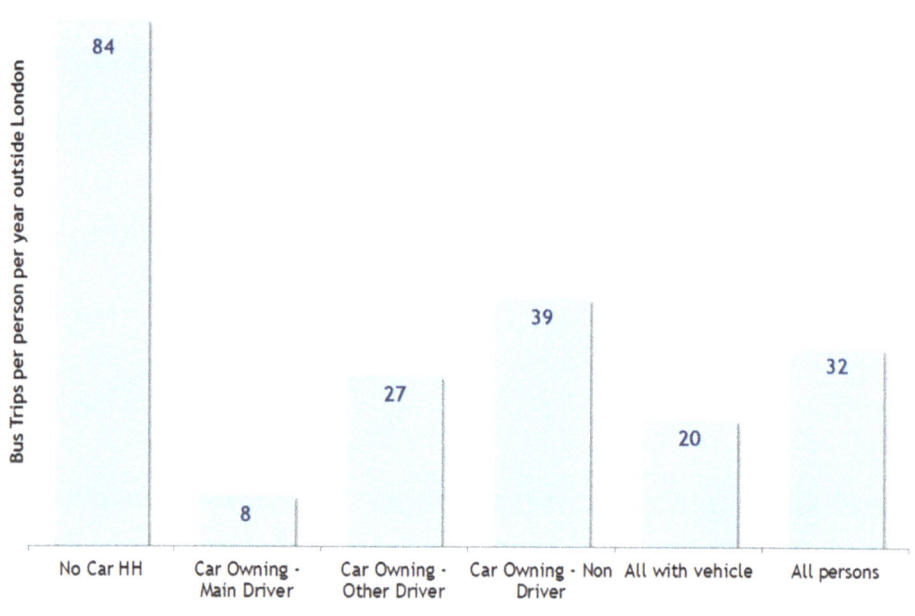

Source: National Travel Survey 2019, Department for Transport

Figure 5-6: Changes in Car Ownership by Region since 1985

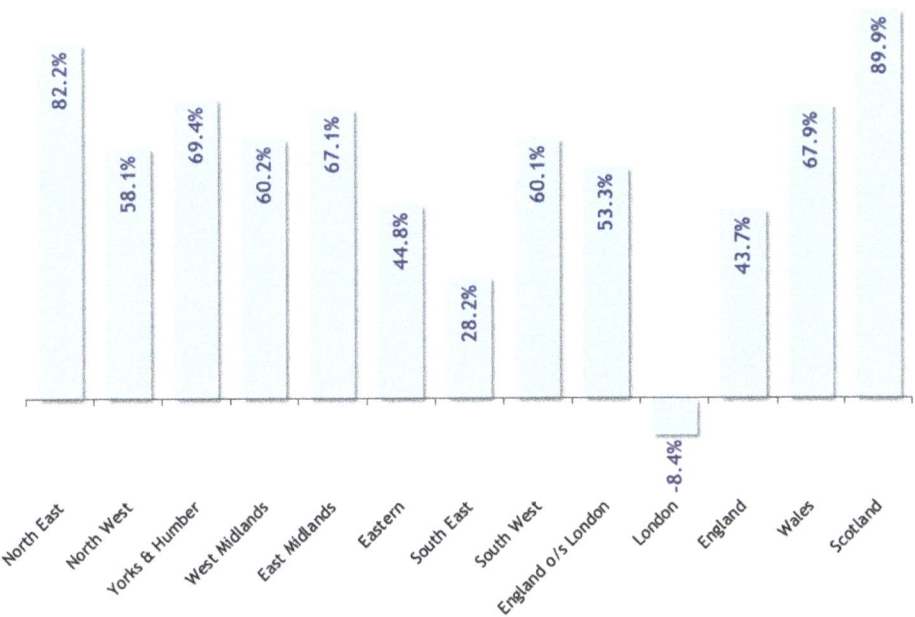

Source: PTIS analysis of statistics published in Transport Statistics Great Britain (DfT), Vehicle Licensing Statistics 2019 (DfT) and Mid-Year Population Estimates (ONS).

substantial indeed in all areas outside the capital. Scotland has led the way, with growth of almost 90%, whilst Wales has experienced growth of 68%. Amongst the English Regions, the fastest growth has been seen in the North East, 82%, with four regions - East Midlands, West Midlands, Yorkshire and the Humber and the South West all seeing growth of more than 60%. London, by contrast, has seen a drop of over eight per cent.

6
Journey Purpose

Introduction

Transport in all its forms is a derived demand: all but the most dedicated enthusiasts do not use transport for its own sake, but as a means to an end. Thus, the market for transport will largely be determined by people's need to travel to work or education, or their desire to travel for other reasons such as shopping, visiting friends and relatives or leisure trips – for example to the cinema, sporting events or other attractions.

Thus, the reasons for travel – and changes in society which result in shifts in those reasons – will have a decisive effect on the volume and timing of demand.

Analysis Tools

The Department for Transport's annual National Travel Survey identifies and asks questions about seven principal reasons for travel:
- Commuting
- Business
- Education (including as escort)
- Shopping
- Personal business
- Other journeys as escort
- Leisure trips

The Relative Importance of Each Purpose

The 2019 NTS shows continuing shifts in the relative importance of different journey purposes - and we can see from the separate analysis for bus in London, that there are significant differences between the two.

Until a few years ago, shopping was the pre-eminent reason for travelling by bus, often accounting for 30% of journeys. By 2019, its importance had diminished considerably.

In London, commuting was now the most important reason,

Figure 6-1: Journey Purpose of Bus Trips in England, 2019

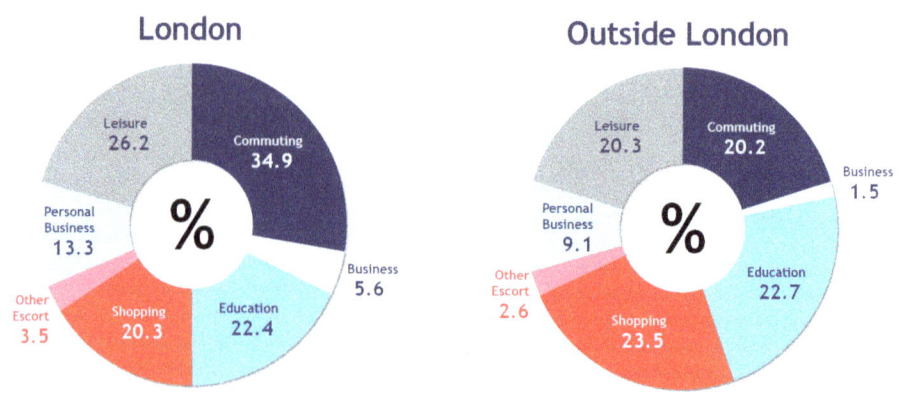

Source: PTIS analysis of National Travel Survey 2019, DfT.

Figure 6-2: Changes in London Bus Trips by Purpose

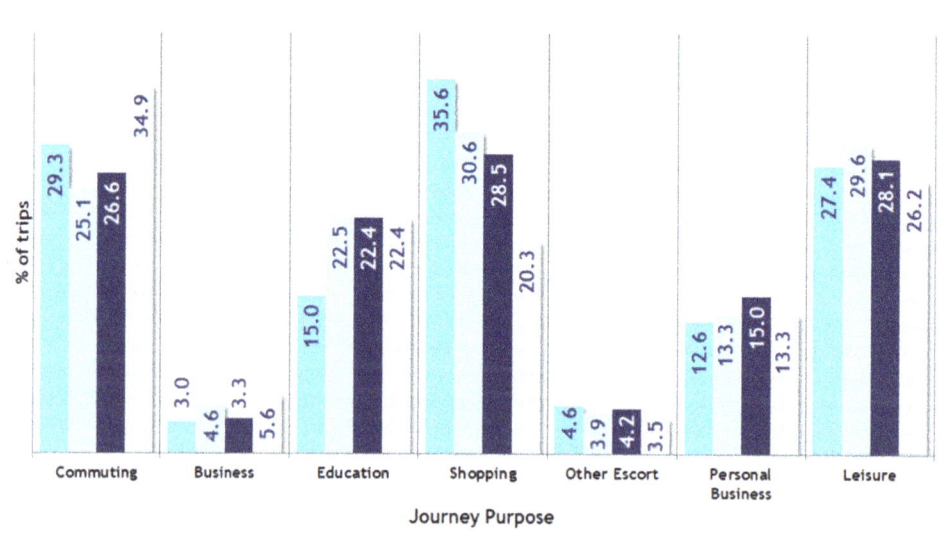

Source: PTIS Analysis of National Travel Surveys 2002, 2007 2012 and 2019, DfT.

accounting for more than a third of all journeys in 2019, followed by travel for leisure purposes on 26.2%. Education was third on 22.4% and shopping now fourth on 20.3%.

Outside the capital, shopping was still the most important on 23.5%, closely followed by education on 22.7%, with leisure trips third on 20.3%. Commuting was fourth on 20.2%. The figures are illustrated in the graph opposite at Figure 6-1.

Changes in Journey Purpose

Looking back to the early part of the last decade, it is possible to see how the pattern of trip making and demand has changed in response to the profound economic and social changes which society over the last twenty years.

The key trends may be summarised as:
- a significant decline in the importance of shopping trips, which accounted for around 30% of bus journeys until the onset of the recession. By 2017, this had fallen to 23.6% - we estimate that this means a loss of some 260 million bus trips a year - almost 6% of the total market.
- A recovery in the use of the bus for work and business trips, which by 2017 and risen over 24% of the total - overtaking shopping as the main reason for bus use.
- Other leisure trips also grew in importance from 2002 onwards, overtaking work trips in 2007, again in 2012 and in 2016, though falling back again in 2017.

The changes in patronage by journey purpose in London since 2002 are illustrated in the chart at Figure 6-2 opposite , which looks at a snapshot of the figures in 2002, 2007, 2012 and 2019. A similar analysis for the areas outside London is shown in Figure 6-3 overleaf.

Figure 6-3: Changes in Non-London Bus Trips by Purpose

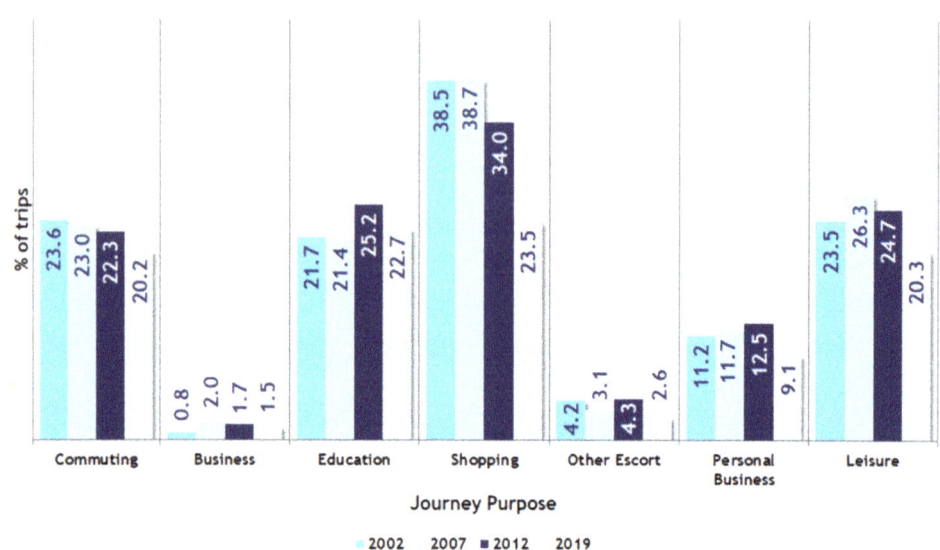

7
The Bus Product

Overview

It is important to understand that each bus journey that people take has several different components, each of which can influence the decisions that consumers make about whether to use the bus, and – where they have a choice – which bus to use.

There are six aspects of bus service provision, or "product attributes", which are of major importance:

- Getting to the Stop

    The time taken to walk from home to the bus stop and from the bus stop to the ultimate destination. Known also as "access time".

- At the Bus Stop

    The time spent at the bus stop waiting for the bus to arrive. Referred to as "waiting time".

- On the bus

    The duration of the ride on the bus from leaving the boarding point to arriving at the alighting point. Also referred to as "journey time" or "in-vehicle time" [IVT])

- Getting from the Stop

    The time taken to walk from the bus stop to the ultimate destination. Also forms part of "access time".

- Price

    The money cost of using the service, paid to the driver or prepaid in the form of a day, weekly or season ticket.

- Quality

    Perceptions of the quality of the service provided – this "umbrella" heading covers such issues as driver behaviour and vehicle quality.

Getting to the Bus Stop

It is important that bus services are close to the residential areas and the other facilities which they are trying to serve. This will minimise the distance that people need to walk in order to get to a bus stop, or from the bus stop to their destination.

Department for Transport statistics[3] suggest that, across England as a whole, 93% of the population is within 600 metres of a bus stop. At a typical walking speed of 3.1 mph, 600 metres will be a walk of just over four minutes for most people.

In urban areas, the proportion rises to 96%, but in smaller towns and on the urban fringe, the proportion falls to 89%, dropping to 72% in rural areas.

In all cases, customers' willingness to walk will be affected by such issues as weather, topography and personal security – safe walking routes in residential areas and good street lighting are vital.

Poor urban design, especially in the fifties and sixties, meant that pedestrian routes were often unsafe, whilst poor road design, especially on developments primarily designed for the private car, can make it impossible to serve residential areas or out-of-town retail developments adequately.

Waiting for the Bus

The time spent standing at the bus stop waiting for the bus to come along is a very important part of the overall journey experience.

People find standing around waiting at stops boring and uncomfortable – especially if the weather is bad. Thus, good, high-quality waiting facilities that are well-maintained to protect people from bad weather are a very important element of the bus product.

Customers tend to perceive the amount of time they must wait to be longer than it actually is – though, as with the journey time, the advent of smartphones has changed that equation radically.

As with journey time, though, reliability is an important factor. Customers find it very annoying when scheduled bus services do not turn up or arrive very late. Real-time information systems either at the

---

[3] *National Travel Survey 2017 Table NTS0801, Department for Transport*

stop or available through smartphones can be a major factor in offering reassurance and confidence to customers – but they must be accurate and reliable in their predictions.

On the Bus

As we saw earlier in our discussion of industry costs in Chapter 2 above, bus speeds and journey times are crucial in determining how much it costs to provide a service. However, they are also critical for customers: how long the journey takes will have a decisive effect on how consumers view a bus service and decide whether they will use it or not.

Bus journeys often seem to be slow, as the vehicle keeps stopping to pick up and set down passengers, has to wait at traffic lights and junctions and – most of the time – sit in the same traffic jams as other vehicles. Indeed, surveys show that the proportion of the time a bus is moving is surprisingly low (see worked example overleaf).

The improved design of bus interiors, coupled with the advent of smartphones and free wi-fi, has transformed the in-vehicle experience for most customers in the past few years. Thus, time spent on a public transport vehicle may no longer be viewed as 'wasted' as it might have been to previous generations – and indeed may be more productive than it is for car drivers.

The predictability of the journey time is a vital factor in the equation, but is too often overlooked. In the surveys undertaken for our worked example overleaf, the average time taken was the advertised journey time of 37 minutes. However, the 45 journeys surveyed showed a variability of time between the fastest at 28 minutes and the slowest at 49 minutes.

This unpredictability undermines customers' trust in the product and in the bus company. Traffic congestion is unpredictable, and other events can intervene as well, so if a bus is late or the journey takes longer, it is not always the bus company's fault, but it is impossible for the customer to distinguish between the causes.

If the bus sometimes takes 50 minutes, then it is likely that the customer will assume that it will always take the longer time and plan accordingly – especially for time-critical journeys like getting to work. Thus, the journey will be perceived as taking 50 minutes even if that only happens once or twice a week.

Worked Example: Delays on an Urban Bus Route

The chart at Figure 7-1 below shows the typical components of an urban bus journey, based on actual surveys of journeys on a major corridor in an English city. The journey length is around 9.6 kilometres, and the average total journey time was 36.7 minutes. Thus, the average speed was 16 kph (9.9 mph) – at the lower end of the range of typical bus speeds we discussed in Chapter 2 above.

It will be seen that typically the bus was only moving for 61% of the time, being stationary for the rest, for a variety of reasons. Getting passengers on and off the bus accounted for almost 16% of the time, whilst being stuck in traffic jams accounted for a similar proportion of the time. Other reasons included waiting at traffic lights, waiting to pull away from stops and waiting at the stop for the correct time for departure.

Figure 7-1: Typical Components of an Urban Bus Journey

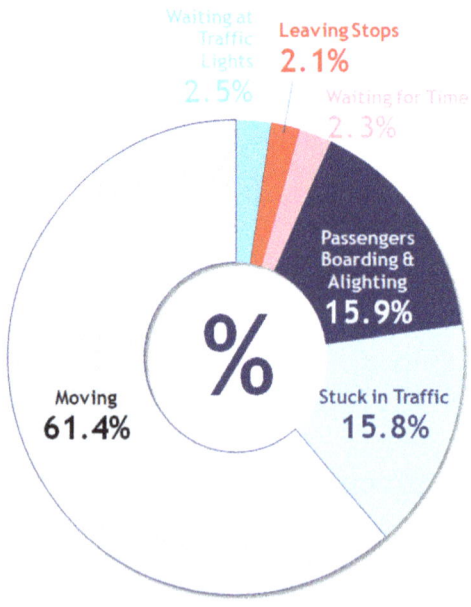

Source: Delay surveys undertaken by The TAS Partnership, 2014.

Price

Fares are payable for all journeys with discounts for regular travellers. Bus fares need to take account of all operating costs. We will consider the question of fares and ticketing in more detail in Chapter 10 below.

Quality

Whilst it is possible to measure and quantify most aspects of bus service provision, there is always the magical extra ingredient which is called "quality".

For the bus operator, there are three main elements to the quality equation: the vehicles, the driver and the overall 'image'.

Vehicles need to be clean, comfortable, and well-maintained. Cleanliness is very important – there is very little point in investing in high-specification leather seating and more up-market floor covering if the bus is strewn with litter when the customer gets on, or the floor has not been mopped for several days.

Comfort is important too – and this embraces the behaviour of the driver in the quality of the ride he or she provides as much as in the design of the seat itself.

The driver – and indeed all the company's customer-facing staff – need to be welcoming, helpful and friendly. The inter-action between driver and customer is the fulcrum on which the whole industry rests: one grumpy driver can drive away customers, spoil his employer's reputation and undo years of hard work in changing political and policy-making attitudes towards the bus. It is difficult to overstate the importance of this, especially in the era of social media.

The overall image projected by the local operator is very significant in changing and managing perceptions of how bus services are viewed by customers and stakeholders. Being able to project a successful, professional, high-quality bus operation in a town or city is very powerful indeed – affecting the overall 'feel' of the place, in understanding and addressing the problems that arise from time to time, and in developing and implementing long term pro-public transport investment and policy. There are many examples of this from around the UK, including cities such as Brighton, Oxford, Nottingham and Edinburgh.

Figure 7-2: The Generalised Cost of a Typical Bus Journey

Figure 7-3: Generalised Cost Components of a Bus Journey

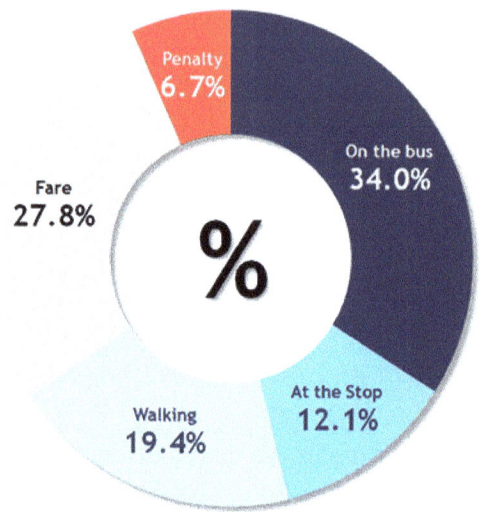

Source: PTIS model

Putting it Altogether

In seeking to understand how people evaluate the product attributes we have discussed so far in this chapter, economists and modellers have evolved the concept of **Generalised Cost**.

An understanding of this concept is an important tool in understanding the effects of competition between modes and within modes – and how people react and change their behaviour as a result.

The theory holds that:
- Generalised cost measures the total cost of a journey including both the price and the time taken from door to door.
- For any given journey, the choices that consumers make about how to travel will be determined by comparing the generalised costs of the different modes available.
- Consumers may be expected, as a rule, to choose what they perceive to be the cheapest.

We show how this works in diagrammatic form in Figure 7-2 above. The breakdown of the cost of a typical local bus journey are shown in Figure 7-3. Note that we refer in that chart to a "penalty" – this is discussed in more detail in Table 1 below.

Where end to end journeys require passengers to change from one bus to another, the journey time needs to reflect both the time taken the waiting time for the second vehicle. To reflect the fact that passengers generally dislike changing buses, the generalised cost will need apply what is referred to as an "interchange penalty" (typically expressed as ten extra minutes).

As well as providing an understanding of the actual costs of a bus journey for customers, generalised cost is used to understand and predict how customers choose their method of travel for different journeys – their **mode choice**.

Mode choice modelling is a highly detailed and complex process which relies on customer research, a detailed understanding of the current pattern of demand for transport and a series of assumptions about the future. This cannot be covered by a book such as this. What we can do, though, is try to help non-modellers understand the process, and how useful an understanding of the concepts can be in making every day commercial and operating decisions.

How Generalised Cost works

Generalised cost is expressed as time in minutes. The cost of the fare is converted into a number of minutes based on estimates of the value of time. Values are derived from survey work around the country.

A good starting point is to consider the components of a bus journey we illustrated in Figure 7-3 above and how they compare with a similar journey by private car. This is done in the table below.

Values and assumptions used in transport appraisal and the models which support it are constantly updated following customer research and to reflect changing circumstances. Our worked example uses a composite value of time of £6.28 per hour. Further information about this complex subject can be found on the web site for the Department for Transport's Transport Assessment Guidance (WEBTAG), at https://www.gov.uk/guidance/transport-analysis-guidance-webtag.

Table 1: Understanding Generalised Costs

Item	Car	Bus	Remarks
Access Time 1	Nothing from home to the car, as this is parked outside.	Getting to the bus stop. Distances to stops are typically up to 400m (5 minutes' walk) which compares with a car parked on the drive.	The walk is affected by such issues as weather and personal security. This results in walk times being perceived typically as twice the actual time
Waiting time	Does not apply	The time spent waiting at the stop can be a significant proportion of total journey times, particularly when services are relatively infrequent or journey times are short.	Affected by Issues like: • weather • personal security • uncertainty about bus arrival. In calculating generalised costs, wait time is taken as half the frequency. However, perception is that wait time seems a lot longer, so minutes are valued at twice actual. Uncertainty can be reduced by real-time information at the stop or via smartphone

Item	Car	Bus	Remarks
In vehicle time	The time actually in the vehicle travelling from A to B.	Bus travel times are usually longer. Factors which lengthen journeys include: • frequent stops • boarding/alighting • collecting fares • traffic congestion	Unpredictable congestion will cause higher perceptions of journey time: people will plan their journey to take account of the worst case, in order to avoid being late for work or missing a connection
Access Time 2: Getting to final destination	Walk from the car park to the ultimate destination. Will be determined by car park location	Generally assumed to be 400m (5 minutes' walk). Can be affected by the bus's ability to provide good access to town/city centres and other key destinations	As before, walk times are generally perceived as being twice the actual time.
Money cost	The cost is usually perceived as the petrol and any parking charge. Other ownership costs are usually disregarded for individual journeys	Fares are payable for all journeys with discounts for regular travellers. Bus fares need to take account of all operating costs.	Importantly, car costs are shared by all the vehicle occupants whereas each bus user pays. Money cost is calculated by using the DfT's value of time in £ per hour.
Quality Penalty	Does not apply	Reflects the 'hassle' factor of using the bus, including the poor perception that non-users have of the product.	Measured by customer research. Can be counteracted by effective marketing and PR.

A Worked Example

This example illustrates the way in which the various components of the generalised cost components are measured, and how the results affects the bus industry's competitive position, which is then discussed in the next chapter.

The example is based on a corridor studied in a live project: an origin and a destination are 3.8 miles apart. The two are linked by a bus service every 10 minutes, with a single fare of £2.40. The bus takes 26 minutes and the car 11.4 minutes.

The results of the calculations are illustrated in Figure 7-4 below, from which it will be seen that the total cost of making the journey by bus is estimated at 82.4 minutes, compared with 22.0 minutes by car.

By using a probability calculation, it is possible to estimate how demand for the journey might be split between competing modes. The model predicts that 86.0% of users with a car available will use the car, with 14.0% using the bus.

Figure 7-4: Generalised Costs Compared
Bus versus Car

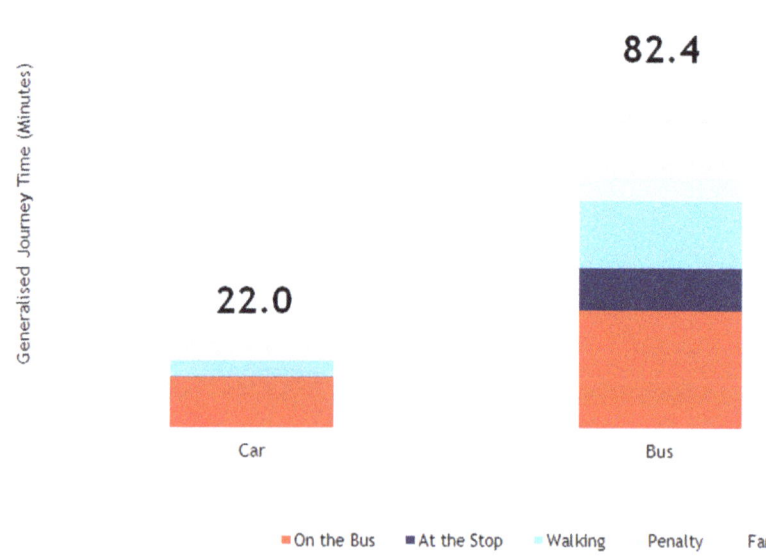

Source: PTIS model

Understanding the Effect of Change

In order to understand the ability - and the limitations - actions to change the generalised cost of public transport use, we have created four scenarios measuring the effect of different policy/commercial options:

a) Bus operators cut their fares by 10%
b) The fare reduction is coupled with a series of bus priority measures and other improvements reduce the overall bus journey time by 30%
c) A competing bus operator enters the market, running two minutes in front of the existing service. Because this creates an uneven frequency of services, it makes but a small difference to the average wait time (the change is assumed to be two minutes). However, the competition forces a 10% fare cut
d) A policy of demand restraint is introduced, increasing the cost of motoring by £2.50 a trip (£5 a day).

The results are illustrated in the graph at Figure 7-5 overleaf.

Under scenario (a), cutting the fares by 10% could increase the mode share of the bus service by around 0.9%. Passenger numbers would rise by around 6%. However, this is unlikely to produce enough additional passengers to fund the loss of revenue caused by the fare cut.

Scenario (b) shows that the provision of bus priority measures and other improvements would reduce the cost of bus travel, and so increase demand, reducing the mode share of the private car by four per cent. If achieved, this would result in a 15% increase in bus demand.

The provision of a competing bus service under scenario (c), operating within two minutes of the existing service, reduces generalised costs compared with the original scenario, but only increases the market share for the bus from 14.0% to 15.7%, increasing bus demand by 12%. This would of course be insufficient to enable the two operators to be profitable, and the competition would not be sustainable. This mirrors the outcome of most competitive situations that have occurred in the industry since 1986.

In scenario (d), the increased charge for motoring rebalances the travel equation significantly, so that the model predicts that the share of trips by car falls from 86.5% to 74.9%, with the balance switching to the bus. This would mean an increase in bus patronage of 78%.

This small example demonstrates the limits of policy that seeks to improve public transport without corresponding action to adjust the costs of using a car.

In the real world, of course, the modelling process is much more complex. For instance, this example is looking at one flow between two fixed points, rather than the complex web of journeys between a wide variety of origins and destinations that a larger model would have to consider.

Nevertheless, generalised cost remains an important tool in understanding customer choice in transport and in estimating the effect of changes, whether it be major projects such as a new tramway or railway line, or the introduction of better bus priority measures.

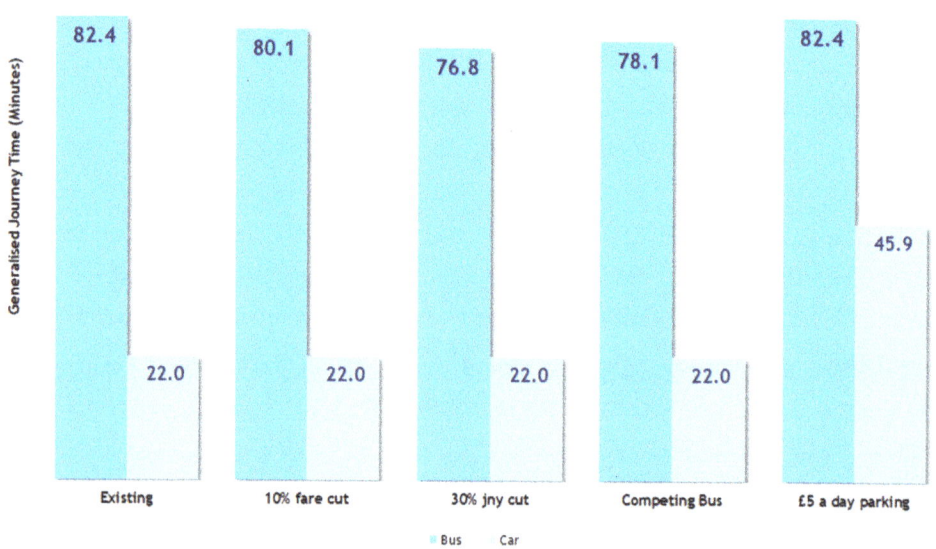

Figure 7-5: Effect of Market Changes on Generalised Costs

Source: PTIS model

8
Keeping the Customer Satisfied

Introduction

The importance of product quality and looking after the customer has long been understood by bus companies and came much more into the forefront of industry managers' minds in the years immediately following privatisation and deregulation. From the early 1970s until 1986, local authorities had become an important source of funding for buses, and their detailed involvement in network planning decisions had meant that the authority, rather than passengers, had become the most important customer. The years after the reforms introduced by the 1985 Transport Act saw a gradual switch in emphasis towards the paying customer.

However, the best practice adopted by some operators has by no means been universal. The result is that, thirty years on, there are wide differences in approaches to and the delivery of customer service.

In 1991, the then President of the UK's Institute of Practitioners in Advertising offered a very succinct definition of marketing which I have used in my analysis work ever since. In the case of the transport industry, though, we need to substitute "services" for goods in his quotation:

> *"First, marketing involves the discovery of what goods customers or potential customers want; second, it involves producing those goods and checking that what has been produced genuinely meets their requirements; third it involves selling those goods at a profit."*

(Winston Fletcher, 1991)

In this chapter we review how Mr Fletcher's definition works in practice for the bus industry. We shall go on to consider the evolution of management styles alongside technological change – particularly the advent of the smartphone and social media.

What Customers Want

Overview – the 'Four Ps' again

Customer desires come in three broad forms, which we examined earlier in the marketing mix diagram discussed in Chapter 4 and illustrated in Figure 4-1 – place, price and product. The fourth 'p' is about promotion – how we reach our customers and potential customers.

Place - Network Design

Bus companies have long understood the importance of customer research in developing and updating their networks. In the 1970s, the National Bus Company (NBC) pioneered some of these techniques in its Market Analysis Project (MAP), a major exercise the understand its customer base and their need and desire to travel by bus.

Demographic analysis, customer research and generalised cost modelling were all used to understand what customers wanted from their local bus networks, and to get to grips with the best way to meet those needs. These techniques were later updated and developed into the "Bus Driver" computer software developed by NBC for use during the run up to the abolition of quantity licensing as part of the deregulation project.

The principles of the research are to establish:
- Where people live (their origins)
- Where they want to travel (their destinations)

A number of methods are employed to do this, by both bus companies themselves and by local transport authorities. They include:
- Continuous surveys of passenger origins and destinations – typically in the larger urban areas
- Analysis of electronic ticket machine data to gain information on origins and destinations (the latter are more difficult to deduce with zonal or flat fares, though this can be done in conjunction with surveys)
- Roadside counts of bus passengers
- Customer research by questionnaire, including travel diaries

Specific addresses are combined into small areas, or zones, so that a pattern of demand can established (a "trip matrix") from one zone to another. Bus routes (or other forms of public transport such as railways or trams) can be planned to meet as many of those needs as possible. The available combinations of routes and frequencies can then be established, and their relative merits tested using the generalised cost techniques we discussed in Chapter 7.

There is no single answer to what an optimum bus network looks like and there are different approaches in different parts of the world to issues such as the need to change buses or modes in order to complete your journey. The availability and cost of resources will also have an impact on the choices made.

Price

As discussed in Chapter 10, research on pricing is an important part of determining companies' fare policies. At its most basic, this takes the form of statistical analysis on the number and type of tickets sold. Prior to the introduction of computers, this was done manually by analysing the waybills completed by drivers and/or conductors. Even quite basic ticket machines from the 1950s and 1960s such as the Setright and London's Gibson machine were fitted with statistical counters to aid this process. This was a labour-intensive and therefore expensive process, however.

With the introduction of electronic ticket machines in the 1990s, much more sophisticated analysis became possible, and several software programs to facilitate this were developed by the ticket machine manufacturers themselves and by third party analysts such as QV Associates and E P Morris. As machines have evolved, so have their data analysis capabilities, and advanced models are able to receive and deliver data in real time. Use of GPS potentially allows origin data to be collected without the need for complex coding of bus stops or fare stages.

More detailed and complex research on fares and pricing is regularly undertaken as part of other customer research projects. In one case, a unique project by FirstGroup in Bristol subjected local bus fares to a major public consultation exercise across the city during 2013. The results enabled the company to redesign its fares and ticketing policy, with very positive results in terms of patronage growth (though not necessarily in profit levels).

Worked Example: Different Approaches to Network Design

Two neighbouring cities are divided into 16 zones. Each seeks a public transport service linking residents from their own zone to all the others as quickly and efficiently as possible. This is illustrated in Figure 81: Two Network Design Illustrations below.

City A opts to provide a direct bus service from each zone to every other zone. The result is a complex network of overlapping routes, some of which may be low frequency depending on the density of population in each zone. However, there is no need to change buses: some might argue that this is more 'customer friendly'.

City B decides that the links from everywhere to everywhere will be provided with a maximum of one change of vehicle. It provides one very high frequency trunk route (the orange route), and a series of feeder routes from four key interchange points (the red circles on the map). The network is simpler and easier to understand, but may be less popular because of the need to change for a high proportion of journeys. It also relies on a high degree of integration, so might not be possible in a competitive environment.

Figure 8-1: Two Network Design Illustrations

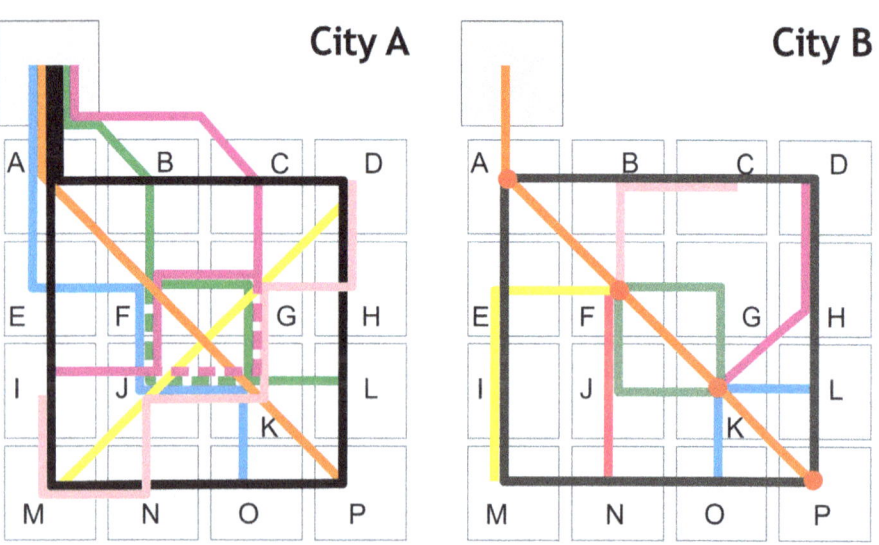

Based on illustrations given in Alan Cannell's book Bus Rapid Transit in Latin America (PTIS, 2008)

Product

Companies, Transport Focus and local transport authorities undertake regular research designed to improve their understanding customer needs and aspirations for their bus service. This can take several forms, including:
- Questionnaires both face to face and web-based
- Focus groups targeted to certain groups of the population, selected by such criteria as age, gender and socio-economic classification
- On-vehicle surveys of existing passengers.

Examples of research regularly undertaken over recent years:
- Non-users – trying to understand what changes or improvements could induce non-users to use bus services
- Young people – establishing the issues faced by young people in using bus services – such as driver attitudes, ticket prices and product complexity
- Women – understanding barriers to women using buses, including such issues as personal security – which can be an issue on vehicles, at bus stops or in walking to and from the bus stop.

Professionals involved in this type of research are convinced of its value in measuring and understanding customer needs and aspirations – as opposed to making assumptions about what they are.

Meeting Customer Requirements

In order to meet Winston Fletcher's criteria, we need measure whether the product we are providing meets the customer's requirements. At its most basic level, the fact that a bus service is well-used and commercially viable is a form of customer research in itself – demand offers a validation, if you like, of the product provided.

However, this is rarely sufficient. The fact that vehicles are constantly on the move makes it very difficult for managers and supervisors to ensure that service delivery is of the right standard and is consistent. This is very different from, say, a factory floor or office environment, where constant supervision can if necessary be provided. Physical production of goods and services has become steadily more automated over the years, which also aids consistency.

Monitoring of service delivery is therefore vital, and there are two principal ways in which this is done:
- Customer satisfaction surveys
- 'Mystery Traveller' surveys

Customer Satisfaction Surveys

This type of survey asks customers either during or immediately after their journey on the bus how satisfied they were with the overall journey experience and with particular aspects of their trip. The biggest and best known survey of this type is that carried out by Transport Focus, the statutory body which has responsibility for representing the interests of users of bus, rail, tram and express coach services – and now also for users of the strategic road network.

The organisation has its origins in the Central Transport Consultative Committee first established to monitor the soon-to-be nationalised railways under the 1947 Transport Act. Originally, a regional structure underpinned the national organisation, but this was abolished by the Railways Act 2005, leaving a single body, which was branded as Passenger Focus in 2005. The organisation's remit was extended to include buses and scheduled coaches in England in 2010.

The bus passenger satisfaction survey was first launched in 2010. It is conducted annually every autumn and has been progressively expanded in terms of sample size and geographical coverage. The autumn 2017 survey covered more than 40,000 bus passengers, who were asked to rate their satisfaction with a wide range of aspects of their journey including:
- the bus stop
- waiting for the bus
- on the bus
- the outside of the bus
- the bus driver

They are also asked for a rating of their overall satisfaction with that bus journey and their rating of value for money it offered.

The satisfaction survey offers several key tools for local managers, local authorities and campaigners:
- geographical benchmarking of individual operators and individual areas one with another

- a trend line in how individual operators are progressing (or not) from one year to another
- a time series measure of quite detailed aspects of the journey experience – cleanliness, for example – which allows managers to identify areas that need improvement, and to monitor the success of steps taken to remedy any deficiencies.

The importance of customer satisfaction surveys, as opposed to more objective measures of service delivery, is that they are measuring the customer perception. And – unfair though it sometimes may seem – perception is everything in customer-facing industries.

The range of responses is quite wide: for example, the autumn 2019[4] survey showed an overall satisfaction range of between 76% and 95% (the percentage of respondents who answered "Satisfied" or "Very Satisfied"). Value for money ratings were between 50% and 77%, whilst punctuality scores fell between 53% and 84%.

---

[4] https://www.transportfocus.org.uk/research-publications/research/bus-passenger-survey/

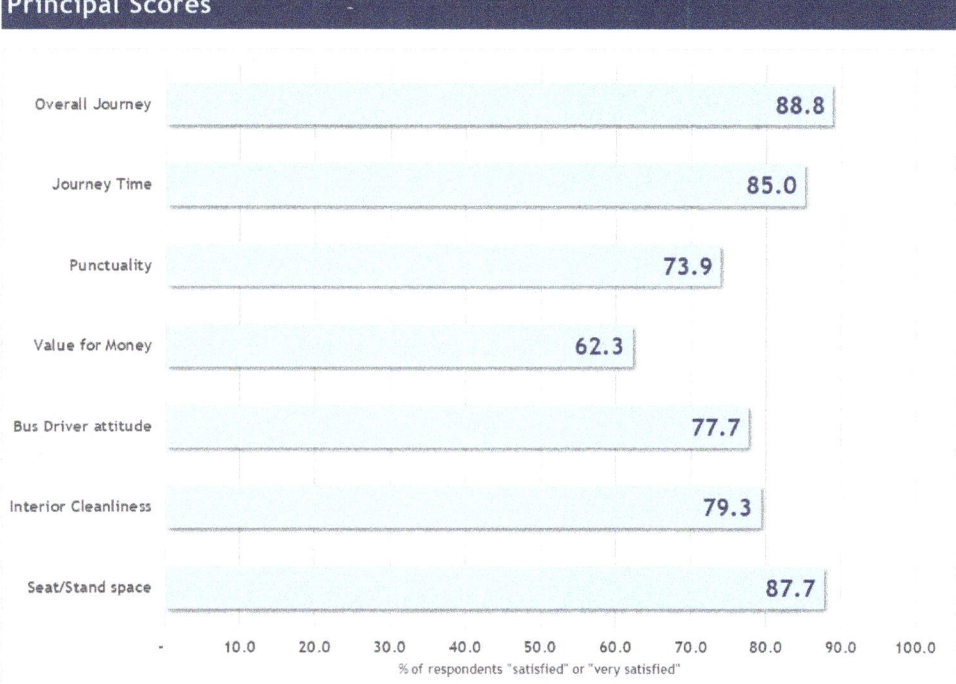

Figure 8-2: Bus Passenger Survey 2019 for England Principal Scores

Overall Journey	88.8
Journey Time	85.0
Punctuality	73.9
Value for Money	62.3
Bus Driver attitude	77.7
Interior Cleanliness	79.3
Seat/Stand space	87.7

% of respondents "satisfied" or "very satisfied"

Source: PTIS Analysis of Scores for major groups, from Transport Focus

In England, the overall scores for 2019 for the five major groups are illustrated in the graph at Figure 8-2 above. Looking back over time, it is noticeable that the scores for each attribute have generally varied by no more than one or two percentage points since 2014. The most notable change has been a continuing rise in the rating for the driver's attitude. This will be welcomed by managers who have put a great deal of effort into improving drivers' customer service skills.

Mystery Traveller Surveys

The concept of using 'mystery shoppers' dates back to the 1940s and originated in the retail industry. The objective is to:
- measure quality of service
- check for compliance with instructions, guidelines or regulations
- gather specific information about products and services.

Mystery shoppers perform specific tasks such as purchasing a product, asking questions, registering complaints or behaving in a certain way, and then provide detailed reports or feedback about their experiences.

For the concept to work well, several conditions are required:
- the mystery shopper's identity and purpose should be unknown
- the assessment should so far as possible be against objective criteria, with a score for each (typically between one and five)
- mystery shoppers need to be trained on how to apply the scoring system consistently and objectively. This is particularly important where several different sites are being checked and compared, or when time series are being used to track changes over time.

The idea of 'mystery travellers' for the bus industry dates back to the early 1990s, including pioneering work done by consultants The TAS Partnership in conjunction with Lancashire municipal operator Hyndburn Transport. After scoring around 50 different aspects of the bus journey, the system used a weighting system derived from market research to identify which aspects were most important to customers. Around the same time, London Buses began similar work, using one of the major market research companies. TAS later operated contracts for the Go-Ahead Group and South Yorkshire PTE, but subsequently withdrew from the market. Other providers then took up the challenge.

The TAS system survived in that it was licensed to the UK Bus

Awards. Though refined and adapted over the years to reflect changing circumstances, it is still used as part of the company's annual assessment of short-listed bus operators, bus depots and drivers.

The Department for Transport instituted a wider system in 2006, which covered the six English PTEs plus Bristol, Leicester and Nottingham. Responsibility for this was transferred to Passenger (now Transport) Focus in 2009, but the survey was discontinued in 2012 following funding cuts.

The concept is still widely used in the industry, though individual methodologies vary and data is not generally published.

The advantage of mystery traveller scores over customer satisfaction scores is their relative objectivity, providing a continuous assessment of the detail of service delivery, without being distorted by customer perceptions or shifting customer priorities.

Mystery travelling is a very useful tool to measure progress and change over time and to benchmark different operations (for example different depots or group subsidiaries).

Customer Information and Communication

The difficulty in getting information about bus services has been a consistent criticism levelled at the industry for many years. There is little doubt that in the early years following bus deregulation, there were major problems as local authorities struggled with their new role in information and infrastructure provision and found great difficulty in keeping pace with rapidly changing route patterns and timetables.

Over the years since, technological developments have driven a complete revolution in passenger information systems. It began with desk top publishing of timetables, then evolved further with the internet, the development of journey planning systems and then the provision of real-time information both at stops and latterly on smartphones. The development of smartphones also powered the growth of social media, which have developed into a powerful communication tool for public transport operators.

This section reviews some of the principal developments.

Travel Information and Journey Planning

For many years, information was limited to timetables, printed in leaflet or booklet form and distributed to the public either free or for a small charge. Many are still produced, either by operators or local transport authorities, and they continue to be an important source of information for a high, albeit diminishing, proportion of passengers. According to the Transport Focus Bus Passenger Survey, 45% of passenger still used paper timetables to get their information in 2014. In 2017, the proportion using printed material was still as high as 36%, but by 2019 it had reduced to 24%. All the resources poured into the development of internet-based information services and apps seemed to be paying off, with the proportion of passengers using them at 31% in 2019, up from just 14% in 2014 and 23% in 2017.

With the advent of the internet, timetables started to appear online, initially as electronic versions of the printed version, using Adobe's Portable Document Format (PDF) which, following its introduction in 1993, became the world-wide standard for document-sharing. An online timetable was the source of information for 42% of people checking bus times before they left home in 2019.

The development of computerised journey planning software began in the late 1980s, using mainframe computers. The advent of the PC enabled the development of systems for personal use, and these were pioneered by railway companies in Holland and Switzerland from 1990 onwards. With the development of the internet, systems began to move online, and the Deutsche Bahn system was rolled out after 1995. In the UK, Transport for London launched the first online multi-modal journey planner in 2001.

Improving information was a key plank of the incoming Labour government's transport White Paper, published in 1998. This contained a commitment to develop a national multi-modal transport information system. As part of that commitment, Traveline was founded in 2000 under an initiative by the Confederation of Passenger Transport (CPT), the UK bus and coach industry trade association. It is a partnership between local authorities and transport operators in the UK to provide impartial and comprehensive information about public transport. As well as providing journey information itself, it also provides timetable and real time bus information to third parties – including Google Maps and Apple Maps – as open data. From 2004, data was also supplied to the Department for Transport's own planner, Transport Direct. The rapid development of private sector systems by transport operators, alongside developers such as Apple and Google led the government to conclude that Transport Direct should be closed, and this happened in 2014.

The provision of data is a major undertaking, requiring the development and maintenance of a register of all the bus stops in the UK – done through the National Public Transport Access Nodes database (NaPTAN), updated daily. This aims to cover every point where public transport of whatever type can be accessed, including railway stations, coach termini, airports, ferry terminals and taxi ranks as well as bus stops. The database has over 360,000 entries. In addition, there is a National Public Transport Gazetteer, which contains around 50,000 place names that may be used to indicate the destination for a requested journey.

Real-Time Information

As congestion started to grow in the late 1950s, it was recognised that the use of automatic vehicle location (AVL) systems would help to manage bus services more effectively, and pioneering work was done in the 1960s in London with the Bus Electronic Scanning Indicator[5]. This used roadside beacons to scan a plate on the side of each bus which gave its route and running number, which was transmitted back to base and enabled route controllers to monitor the position of each bus. A similar system was trialled in Bristol in 1972: in the Marconi "B-Line" system, the beam was on the bus which read a bar code on a plate placed at intervals along the route. However, the vibrations of the bus caused the laser scanners to fail and the system was abandoned.

It took the introduction of mobile phone technology and global positioning satellites to enable the development of systems which were affordable and had the necessary accuracy.

---

5   *For a more detailed description of BESI, please see the London Transport Museum video at https://youtu.be/qGwZwe6izTg*

It was recognised that development of AVL systems would also enable operators to keep the public better informed about how bus services were running – and this led to the development of real-time information systems. This initially displayed information on electronic displays at bus stops, but increasingly is used to route information directly to customers' own computers, tablets and smartphones.

Early experiments in real-time information such as the London Countdown system (1992) relied on beacons to track vehicles and used predictive algorithms to forecast bus arrival times and individual stops. Using GPS improved accuracy in locating vehicles and predicting arrival times at stops. Major roll-outs of systems have occurred including London (which developed the integrated iBus system, installed between 2008 and 2012) and other cities throughout the UK – usually in partnership with or on the initiative of the local transport authority.

With the severe cutbacks in local government funding that have occurred since 2010, there has to some extent been a loss of momentum with some systems being reduced in coverage and others (for example in Lancashire) being shut down altogether. At the same time, however, the development and spread of smartphone apps has enabled the real-time data to be distributed more quickly and cost-effectively.

Data from Transport Focus suggests that amongst those who checked bus departure times before setting off for the stop, 31% used a live position update in 2019, up from 23% in 2017 and just 14% in 2014. Meanwhile, use of online timetable information has increased from 35% in 2014 to 42% in 2019. Online users exceeded paper timetable users from 2017 onwards.

The Internet and Social Media

Alongside the development of journey planning systems, the rapid growth of the internet and mobile phone technology revolutionised the way in which business could be in touch with its customers – through mass e-mails, SMS text messages and social media websites.

The mainstays of the modern social media developments, Facebook and Twitter, were both founded in 2006, and their growth was powered by the development of the mass-market touch-screen smartphones. The Apple iPhone was launched in 2007, and the first Android-powered phone followed fifteen months later.

From the bus industry's point of view, social media has enabled:
- Rapid communication of problems and disruptions to service
- The opportunity to build a community amongst its customers
- The development of marketing opportunities for new or updated ticketing products, new routes and service changes and other added value products.

Go-Ahead Group subsidiary Metrobus was amongst the earliest UK operators to develop the use of social media in 2008, and others quickly followed.

There is little doubt that establishing a strong social media presence has been successful for many bus operators. However, managing a successful presence of this type requires a significant investment – particularly in people. This means having sufficient resources to cover the majority of the service day, and in training them to have the right skills for the job.

The conditions for success rely on:
- Keeping it local – knowledge of the network and the geography is essential – using a remote 'call centre' approach tends not to work
- Frequent communication – a programme of positive news stories, special offers and other posts to keep customers engaged
- Rapid notification to customers of problems, requiring close liaison with operations staff and/or controllers (another reason for keeping it local)
- Rapid responses to complaints/comments
- A nuanced and balanced use of language, especially in the case of complaints and grumbles – sufficiently informal and friendly to appeal to the target audience and avoiding the use of officialese or defensive language.

Conclusion: Customers at the Heart of the Business

Putting the customer at the heart of a business, making sure the customer genuinely comes first, the need to delight customers – all phrases that have become almost clichés over the last couple of decades in a whole range of businesses. In many cases, they have genuinely come to mean something to companies and their staff. In others, though, a failure to follow through and deliver has made a mockery of the whole concept.

Customer focus is to a large extent a matter of company culture, and change can take a long time to work through an organisation. Culture is a product of history as much as anything, with attitudes and approaches being passed through successive generations of staff without the knowledge or influence of management.

Decisive intervention in the form of training, an eye for detail and strong leadership are three key factors in change management. Follow-through is important, too, so that both customers and staff can see that there is real meaning in the change, rather than paying lip service to the idea.

Companies which have succeeded commercially – with high levels of ridership, a track record of growth and strong local reputations – are those which have succeeded in delivering a genuine customer-first ethos.

Managers who lead effectively are the ones who really know their local network, can be seen riding on their buses, and genuinely engage with staff and customers at terminal points and in depots, who take a close interest in standards of presentation in offices and on vehicles.

Bus companies who use the full range of tools we have described in this chapter are the ones who succeed. For a whole variety of reasons, that success has become progressively harder to achieve in recent years, but even in periods of falling patronage, such businesses tend to be able to mitigate decline, and have a larger base from which to recover.

9
Competition

Overview

Competition in the bus industry in the UK is often thought of as competition between bus operators for market share, often in 'bus war' situations where operators compete directly for passengers on the street.

However, this is not the case: the main competition for most bus services is from other forms of transport, mainly the private car but also walking or cycling, or – increasingly – not travelling at all. Other forms of public transport, such as rail or light rail are competitors for some specific journeys or on some corridors. Taxi and private hire cars, either operating as hail and ride or via computer-based networks such as Uber or Lyft are also perceived as significant competitors.

The Demographic Challenge

As the analysis of bus passengers above shows, buses rely on key demographic groups, including non-car owners, young people and older people for the bulk of their patronage – particularly outside London.

The fact is that, for a variety of reasons, the number of people in each of these groups is in long term decline:

- The number of households without access to a car continues to fall.
- The number of young people in the country has been falling and will continue to do so until the end of this decade. A rise in the birth rate in the years immediately after the turn of the century will reverse this trend for a few years.
- Amongst older people, firstly, the proportion of retired people with access to a car is rising, and the volume of travel by retired people has been falling – even since the introduction of free concessionary travel

Thus, the industry's core markets continue to erode, and the risk is that, eventually, they will be too small to support commercially viable services in all but a very few areas. Meanwhile the industry needs to maintain and increase its revenue in order to fund existing levels of service and investment in the future.

The only alternative is to seek growth by attracting car users to make more journeys by bus – and this is where an understanding of the competitive position of the bus, and the disadvantages from which it suffers, becomes so important.

External Competition

Consumers often have a choice of competing external modes when it comes to deciding how they will make their journeys. Increasingly, too, they will have enticing reasons for not making the journey at all, and – through the internet – the means of avoiding the need to make the trip.

Walking

Consumers may choose to walk. For shorter journeys, this choice becomes more likely, because it is possible to reach the destination directly within the time they might have to wait for public transport to arrive. However, this option is affected by weather and by the age and mobility of the consumer. Free travel passes, or network tickets such as Travelcards where there is no fare for the journey, also influence the choice.

Cycling

Cycling is a potential alternative. It requires the purchase and maintenance of a bike, and it is not appropriate for all journeys. However, on a point to point basis it is often faster than a bus service when walking and waiting are considered. Decisions about cycling will also be affected by facilities such as cycle lanes and parking facilities at the destination. Recent extensive investment in infrastructure, particularly in London, has made a significant difference.

In markets where the cycling culture is established – such as Copenhagen, the Netherlands and (closer to home) cities such as Oxford and Cambridge – cycling has proved itself to be a significant competitor to the bus. Both travel modes are often travel choices for those who are environmentally aware.

The combination of extra investment, growing popularity and environmental awareness has resulted in a 30% increase in the volume of travel by bicycle over the last decade, according to Department for Transport statistics. However, cycling's modal share still represents less than one per cent of total travel demand.

Private Cars

As we have already seen, cars are a significant competitor to buses, particularly when a consumer has exclusive access to one. The actual and (more importantly) perceived advantages of using cars are outlined in Table 1 above.

If people have a car available for a trip, they are much less likely to choose the alternative of bus or walking, and the worked example illustrating the relative costs of a typical local journey in section above explains why.

Taxi and Private Hire Vehicles

One mode mirrors the comfort and convenience of the private car, and that is the taxi. The arrival of smartphone-driven applications such as Uber and Lyft have meant that much attention has been focused on the taxi/private hire market in recent years. They have been perceived by many as a threat to public transport modes in general.

Taxis have a number of competitive advantages, including the lack of regulation of driving hours and the fact that charges are levied per journey and not per person. Thus, where a group of two or more people is travelling together, there is often a price advantage over the bus.

Statistics on taxi use are not kept and are therefore difficult to find. Over the years bodies such as the Competition Commission and the Law Commission have used data from the National Travel Survey and regular consumer spending statistics published by the Office for National Statistics to provide estimates of the size of the market. However, this approach does of necessity omit the incoming tourist market, which is an important component of demand, and therefore is likely to understate the total.

There is some evidence from the National Travel Survey of increase in demand in recent years, after a fall in the early years of the century.

The surveys showed a fall in trips per person per year in England from 11.6 or 11.7 in 2002 and 2003 to below 10 in the aftermath of the 2007 financial crisis, thereafter see sawing between 9.9 and 10.5, until a sudden dip to 9.1 in 2017. Multiplying this up by the population suggests a trip volume of around 595 million in 2017, rising to 706 million in 2019 before the onset of Covid-19.

Expenditure surveys suggest that the total income of the taxi and private hire industry in England is around £3.4 billion – up from around £2.9 billion in 2015 and 2016. These figures are after adjustment for inflation to 2018/19 prices using the Consumer Price Index (CPI). These figures include some estimates for the incoming and business markets, using a methodology set out in our report *The Bus Demand Jigsaw 2020*. These estimates suggest that the average revenue per trip would be around £5.36, 24% lower than the run up to the 2007 financial crisis.

Not Travelling at All

Finally, as already mentioned, not travelling at all is also a choice. This is particularly true for those whose journeys are optional, such as for shopping or leisure – but increasingly it also can affect commuting as well. Thus:

- Shopping trips can be switched to the on-line alternative (reaching 20 per cent of all retail sales pre-Covid and since rising to over 30 per cent).
- People who make leisure journeys have the alternative of staying at home, and spending their time in other ways, such as watching television, playing computer games, or surfing the web.
- The growth of the internet and particularly high-speed broadband means that working from home is an option for an increasing proportion of the workforce.

Conclusions on External Competition

For a market to operate and serve customers successfully, the enterprises involved need to be truly market-oriented, and to undertake "marketing" in its widest sense.

Bus operators in a commercial environment generally wish to operate services to generate enough profit to provide appropriate levels of return and to meet their financial obligations. As we have seen, this has been difficult in the falling market that the industry has experienced for the last 50 years.

However, as with all industries, there are outstanding examples of success, particularly in cities such as Brighton, Oxford, Cambridge and Nottingham, and we would argue strongly that these successes have resulted primarily from bus companies and local authorities working in partnership over many years to deliver the maximum possible benefit to passengers by reducing the generalised cost of the bus journey, and rebalancing the generalised cost equation away from the private car.

In this way:
- the quality of the bus journey has been driven up
- the fare has been restrained or even fallen (because rising volumes spread the costs of operation over a greater number of passengers)
- the community has benefited from lower levels of congestion and pollution.

Internal Competition - Other Bus Services

Context

In addition to the much more important competition from cars and other private forms of transport, there is potential for competition between different bus services.

Since 1986, bus operators in Great Britain outside London have been able to compete with each other with minimal restrictions. Whilst there have been some legislative changes since, these have not materially affected the ability of bus operators to compete with one another. Indeed, some legislative changes have been made that were designed to improve operators' ability to do so.

Competition in the bus industry is based on the premise of 'choice' and its proponents believe that it leads to lower prices and better services. Since 1986, this view has generally taken by competition authorities, who have treated bus services as a distinct product, with little regard to the potential effects of bus service competition on what the industry would see as the more significant competition with other modes.

The Difference between Transport and Other Goods/Services

Three particularly important factors make it difficult to treat transport products like other consumer products, and require special consideration:

- Firstly, the instantly perishable nature of the industry's product, which can be characterised basically as a seat available between point A and point B at a given time. If it is not occupied or sold immediately, it has gone and cannot be recovered: but the operator has still borne the cost of producing it.
- Secondly, the fact already discussed that demand for transport is derived demand. Transport is a means to an end (going shopping for example or getting to work, school or college or just meeting up with family or friends)
- Thirdly, there is the question of time, which is an extra dimension in the demand equation.

The Importance of Time

Consumers make their choices when buying goods and services on the basis of price and quality, but in the case of transport, time adds third dimension to the equation. As we have seen in Chapter 7, time can be accounted for in a calculation of generalised cost, but if observers consider consumer behaviour based on price alone, then choices may seem to be perverse and apparently irrational.

Take, for example, consumer behaviour when two or more bus operators are competing on the same route. Customers almost always choose to get on the first bus that comes along, rather than wait for one that might be cheaper or offer better quality. Observers have been puzzled since bus deregulation reintroduced competition to the market in 1986.

However, when you consider that decision in terms of generalised cost, it becomes entirely rational, because the additional wait time at the stop outweighs any saving from a lower fare or any benefit from a better or more comfortable bus.

The following worked example considers the journey point covered by our generalised cost example we looked at in Chapter 7.

Worked Example: The Effect of a Competing Bus Route

It will be recalled that our model considers an origin and a destination 3.8 miles apart. The two are linked by a bus service every 10 minutes, with a single fare of £2.40. The bus takes 26 minutes and the car 11.4 minutes. The bus has a total cost of 82 minutes, and the mode choice model predicts a market share of 14%.

In the competing bus scenario, a new competing bus service is introduced, running two minutes ahead of the existing service and cutting the fare by 10%, forcing the incumbent operator to follow suit.

Therefore, the average wait time is reduced to eight minutes, and the fare falls to £2.16. The result is a fall in the generalised cost of the bus mode from 82.2 minutes to 78.1. The model suggests that the mode share of the bus would rise from 14% to 15.7%, increasing bus patronage by 12%.

If customers got on the first bus that came along, available patronage would be split evenly between the two companies. That would leave the original operator with only around 56% of the passengers that were using his buses before the competitor started to run (50% of the original number, plus half the 12% gain).

Given that the original operator was previously making a profit in line with his cost of capital, the loss of 44% of his revenue would make the route unprofitable. Thus, he would be faced with three options:

- give up the route (and demonstrate his weakness, so inviting competitors to attack all his other routes)
- respond and attempt to ensure that his opponents' losses are greater than his and the opponent cannot sustain the losses for longer than he can.
- buy the competitor out.

Whatever happens, the competition is not sustainable in the medium or long term.

Conclusions - Barriers to Competition

As we have seen, there are considerable external pressures on bus operators:
- The demographic profile on which they have relied is in long term decline
- Levels of car ownership have risen and are forecast to continue to do so
- Bus speeds are in long term decline as a result of growing congestion, so increasing the costs of operation and reducing the attractiveness of the product
- Profit levels are short of the levels necessary to sustain the long-term investment and financial health of the industry.

In some countries of the world and in some markets, there is almost an unlimited demand for public transport, but this is not the case in most western countries including the UK. Consequently, most new services, whether they cover new markets or replicate existing services, will not become profitable immediately and it may take many months or even years for them to reach break-even levels.

The nature of competition in transport, as we have seen, is pre-eminently about *time*, which is monetised by reference to the concept of generalised cost discussed in Chapter 7 above. This explains why, as the Office of Fair Trading noted in 2009, consumers do not make choices based on price or quality – as they would typically in other markets.

In order to establish a new commercial service, particularly a new competitive service, bus operators therefore need to have significant financial reserves or be prepared to sustain a period of reduced overall profitability. However, given that profit levels in most areas are already well below necessary levels, it is rare that this can be done.

At the same time, incumbent operators will almost always respond to a new market entrant aggressively. This is because, in most cases, the introduction of competition on a corridor will not merely *reduce* profits in the short term, but in most cases *wipe them out completely*.

10
Fares and Ticketing

How fares are determined

Basic Concepts

The four basic ways in which fares are calculated:
- **Distance-Based Fare**: the fare charged rises in line with the distance travelled. Typically, the fare comprises an initial fixed boarding charge, together a charge for the distance travelled. Thus the fare as the journey gets longer, but the charge per unit of distance travelled tends to fall.
- **Flat Fare**: one basic charge for boarding a vehicle, regardless of distance travelled
- **Zonal Fare**: one or more routes is divided into geographical zones with charges set for travel within one zone or between a combination of adjacent zones
- **Time-Based Fare**: Customers buy a ticket which entitles them to travel as many times as they like for a defined period

Historically in the UK, the distance model was the commonest – passengers paid to travel between two points or 'stages'. The charges for that journey were determined on charge per mile or per stage – hence "stage carriage services", the legal name for local bus services until 1985. The distance charge system was also used on the railways when they were built, and subsequently used for the tram networks that became a feature of so many towns and cities in the late 19th and early 20th centuries.

In recent years, the concept of a time-based ticket has become increasingly common, and can be combined with distance, zonal or flat fares. Typical periods cover a single day, a week, a month or longer periods up to a year.

Modern methods of fare collection and payment have, in some cases, blurred the lines between the different methods whilst the introduction of new technology has enabled the introduction of new ticketing products, whilst older products – such as the paper transfer traditionally used in North America – are being abolished.

In the UK, the last two decades have seen a movement away from stage-based fares towards zonal or flat fare systems. Even where stages are still used, the systems have been simplified and the number of stages reduced. In addition, a much lower proportion of passengers pay a stage-based fare on the bus, since most bus users in almost all areas are now using day tickets, period passes and concession passes.

A more detailed discussion about different fare types, and how these compare across the world, can be found in regular National Fare Survey reports published by The TAS Partnership.

Return fares

Traditionally, return fares were offered for services in a stage-based system, usually though not exclusively for longer journeys. However, many operators have abolished return fares, at least for shorter distances and for urban operation – replacing them by day tickets. In the 1960s and 1970s, many operators adopted cheaper return fare offers for journeys undertaken outside the main peak hours, aimed at leisure travellers and, in the days before concessionary travel, older people.

Season Tickets

The railway industry recognised quite early on the benefits of offering season tickets to their regular passengers, both to win their loyalty on competing routes, but also to generate cash flow benefits. The concept dates back at least to the 1860s. Until relatively recently, however, season tickets were limited to specific origins and destinations, offering unlimited travel only between those points for a specified period, which might be a week, a month, a term or a year.

Multi Journey tickets

A more flexible alternative to the season ticket was the multi-journey ticket or the 'carnet', in which a ticket (or a book of tickets) was sold, entitling the user to travel between two points or at a certain fare value a defined number of times without further payment. Many variants of this system were tried in the 1960s and 1970s, and many operators referred to them as "Ten Trip Tickets", offering ten rides for the price of eight or nine. However, fraudulent travel was an issue and the tickets proved difficult to police. The period of high inflation in the early and mid-1970s also caused problems for pre-printed tickets. Some operators and authorities still offer carnet tickets, though the introduction of smartcard systems such as Oyster is rendering them obsolete.

Day Tickets

The idea of day tickets allowing unlimited travel for a specific period on a network or in a specific area has been popular for many years. The London County Council offered a network day ticket in the 1920s, and London Transport followed this with its popular "Red Rover" ticket which offered unlimited travel on the whole of the red bus network.

Other companies adopted similar products, such as Midland Red's "Day Anywhere" ticket, as companies targeted the leisure market. In the 1970s, the National Bus Company's Explorer tickets extended this product to most parts of England and Wales.

Day tickets are now pretty much universal in bus networks across the country, and also for multi-operator ticketing schemes in major cities and conurbations.

Network Tickets

The principle of a ticket which offered unlimited travel on a network for a period longer than a day was pioneered in the UK in the West Midlands, where the Passenger Transport Authority introduced the Travelcard in 1972. Its success meant that the concept quickly spread to other towns and cities around the country, and London followed suit in 1981.

Since then, time-based network-wide products, whether a week or a longer period such as a month or a quarter have expanded rapidly, both in the UK and around the world. Thus, except for a few small operators, virtually all transport systems and individual UK operators now offer some sort of network ticket.

In a flat fare system, the day and period tickets are generally at a fixed price for the service area. In a zonal system, fares for day and period tickets tend to be linked to the number of zones covered, although day tickets in such areas are sometimes at a flat fare covering all zones.

Contactless Smart Cards

The development of the contactless smartcard in the 1990s created the opportunity to develop a product that could be used as an electronic wallet in which a variety of different ticketing products could be stored. Each of the products could be validated using a common protocol, this allowing trip data to be recorded in a uniform format.

The most successful and well-known of these wallets, in the UK at least, has been London's Oyster system, developed from 1998 onwards and rolled out progressively from 2003. Oyster carries several different products, including:

- Travelcards – unlimited travel on all ground-based transport in London in a series of zones, for periods of between one day and one year
- Bus Season tickets – similar products limited to bus and Tramlink services
- Freedom passes – free concessionary travel passes issued to young persons, people with disabilities and people aged 60 and over.
- Pay-As-You-Go – payment of individual fares for journeys undertaken, deducted from an amount of money ("stored value") added to the ticket by the customer. Linked to PAYG are two important features which have added greatly to Oyster's success – "capping" and "auto top-up".
    - "capping" occurs when individual fares paid for journeys taken within a day or a week are only charged up to the price of the appropriate day or weekly ticket, after which journeys undertaken are without additional charge.
    - "auto top up" is where the individual customer consents for an automatic top-up of the amount of cash in the electronic wallet when a defined lower limit has been reached. The sum is automatically charged to the customer's designated bank or credit card and the customer notified by e-mail.

Similar tickets have been rolled out in other areas, and the English National Concessionary Travel scheme (ENCTS) has required the use of standard smartcards since 2010. However, other systems have struggled to replicate London's functionality and speed, so that Oyster remains by far the largest and most successful, with some 34 million cards in issue.

Contactless Bank Cards

The development of the contactless bank card and the parallel use of smartphones as a payment device have both offered new opportunities for transport operators. When working properly both offer significant time savings over cash payment.

The bank cards have an electronic purse which contains £30, which is available for immediate spending without further authorisation. The purse is automatically topped up from the customer's bank account. Because the transactions do not need authorisation at the time of payment, they can be undertaken off-line and only processed at the end of a driver's shift. There is thus no need for the vehicle to be connected to the internet all the time during its journey.

After initial trials in Merseyside with Stagecoach, the first contactless payment cards went live in London in 2012. Since then, contactless payment has been rolled out progressively by bus operators across the country, a process completed during 2020.

The Future

Ticket types and payment systems have evolved rapidly over the last decade, and further innovation in when and how to pay for travel may be expected. In particular, the development of "Mobility As A Service" (MAAS) products will see the integration of bus fares with charges for other modes, including rail, tube, taxi, hire car and cycle hire.

The introduction of the Oyster contactless smartcard system in London was undoubtedly a huge success, though there continue to be concerns about the costs of the back-office systems need to police and distribute the revenue between the operators. There are several barriers to future development in other areas around the cost of processing transactions – an average fare of £1.32 with most operators on a margin of 6-8% does not leave a huge amount of spare cash to pay to third parties in commission or transaction fees.

The abolition of cash fares on London's bus network in July 2014 proved somewhat controversial, provoking concerns about socially disadvantaged people without bank accounts or on low incomes and therefore unable to afford a smartphone or prepay their bus fare. Similar concerns exist in other parts of the country as well, where such people represent a higher proportion of the industry's customers.

However, by the time Transport for London went cashless, only one per cent of all transactions involved a cash payment, and the cost of cash-counting infrastructure could no longer be justified. It was estimated at the time that savings of £24m a year would be achieved as a result.

The question therefore is whether other areas may follow suit. The short answer is "not yet". Prepayment and contactless payment are not yet as well advanced as London, and cash still plays an important if diminishing role in bus operation in other parts of the country. That may well change over time, as operators use differential pricing and other incentives to push more of their customers towards electronic payment systems. At some point, the same tipping point as London may well be reached, when the volume of cash taken cannot support the cost of counting it.

How Fares are Set

The fares charged will be designed by whoever controls the network (a commercial operator or an authority such as Transport for London) in order to raise sufficient revenue to meet a set target:
- In the case of commercial operation, the target will be operating cost plus sufficient surplus to cover the cost of capital.
- Where operations are subsidised, the authority will seek to achieve a given level of passenger revenue, as determined by the authority's agreed budget.

Operators and authorities have historic data about how their revenue is earned – both in terms of the routes they run, but also in terms of the proportion of passengers who pay a given fare.

In order to achieve a given percentage increase in revenue, decisions will be required on how to achieve it: an across-the-board percentage increase, perhaps, or targeted changes in specific fares. Other considerations might include how recently a particular fare value was changed, or the need to incentivise passengers to switch to prepaid tickets.

Drivers of Fare Changes

There are two broad reasons why operators or authorities need to raise more revenue from customers:
- Changes in cost levels – increase in wage costs or fuel prices, for example
- Reductions in passenger numbers – a drop in patronage means that the same level of revenue needs to be earned from fewer people.

Looking at movements in **cost per passenger journey** will provide a better understanding of the need for fare changes than just looking at overall operating costs or trying to apply an unrelated index such as broader inflation measure.

As can be seen from the graph at Figure 10-1 below, these costs rose consistently in real terms from 2005 until 2012, but have fluctuated since, assisted by falls in fuel prices in some years, and continuing low wage increases.

Figure 10-1: Changes in Cost Per Passenger Journey
GB Outside London in Constant (2019/20) Prices

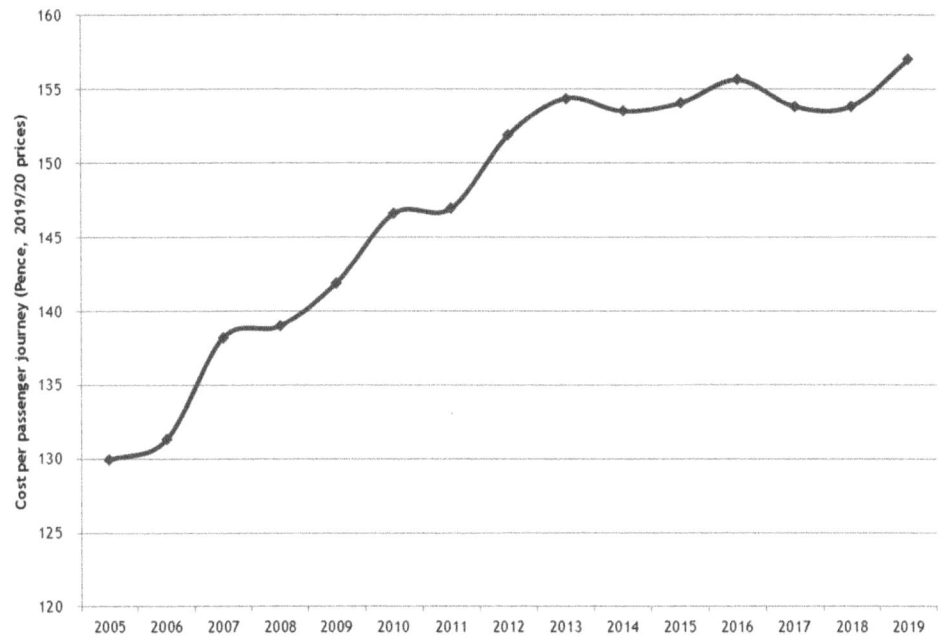

Source: PTIS Analysis of Annual Bus Statistics, Department for Transport, Sheet BUS0407

The total increase since 2005 is 20.9% in Great Britain outside London. Over the last five years, however, the increase restricted to 1.9%. In Scotland and Wales, because of more substantial falls in patronage, the increases have been much larger (51.8% in Scotland and 41.8% in Wales).

Tracking Fare Levels

The DfT tracks fare levels around the country via quarterly bus fares indices. These are prepared from regular surveys of a panel of major operators. The surveys record the percentage change in fares, defined as the variation in the operator's total passenger receipts due to the fares adjustments, assuming that the increases had no effect on passenger numbers; this is also known as the "gross yield".

For many years, the survey and the indices prepared from it were based on individual fares and took no account of multi-journey or day tickets. This was changed after a review of the methodology by the UK Statistics Authority in 2011. However, multi-operator ticket prices were still excluded.

The indices are produced for different parts of Great Britain and can be seen in the graphs at Figures 10-2 and 10-3 opposite. The dips in the indices in England in 2007 and 2010 reflect the effect of the introduction of free concessionary travel and its subsequent extension to be England-wide. The impact was lower in the PTE areas since Merseyside and West Midlands already had free concessionary travel.

In total, over the period since 2004/05, fares in London have risen by 25.5%, whilst in the PTE areas the rise has been 39.8%. In the English Shires, the increase has been lower at 21.4%. Scottish increases have been 27.7%, while Welsh rises have been 21.8%.

Over the five years to 2019, before the onset of Covid, London saw a 4.4% fall, thanks to Mayor Khan's fares freeze. In the PTE Areas, the rise was 4.9% but a higher 8.5% in the English Shires. In Scotland, the rise was 6.7%, whilst in Wales it was just 0.5%.

Average Revenue per Passenger Journey

The trends in revenue per passenger journey (average fare paid) are shown in Figure 10-4 for England and Figure 10-5 for Scotland and

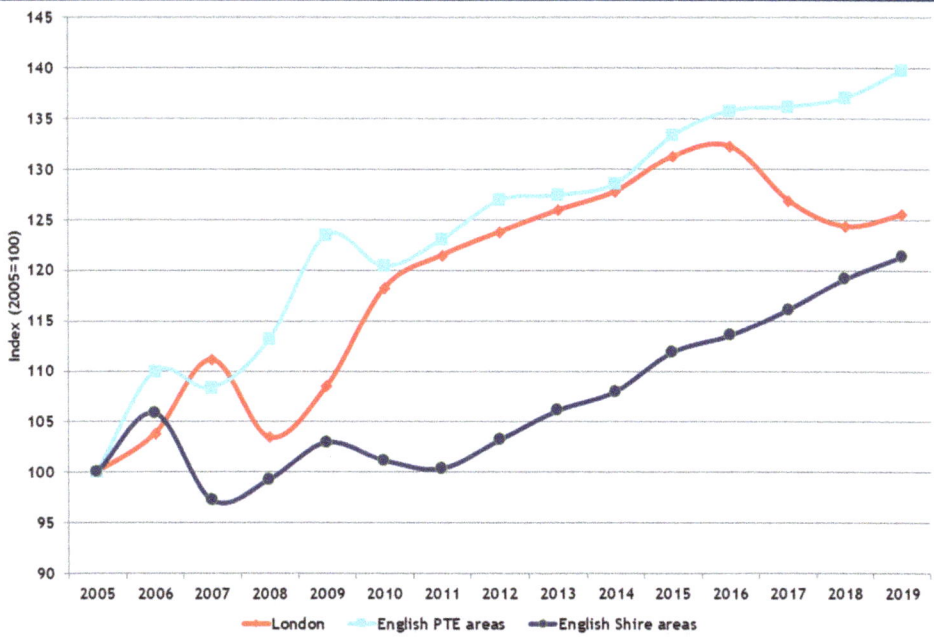

Figure 10-2: Real-Term Fares Indices since 2005
London, PTE Areas and English Shires

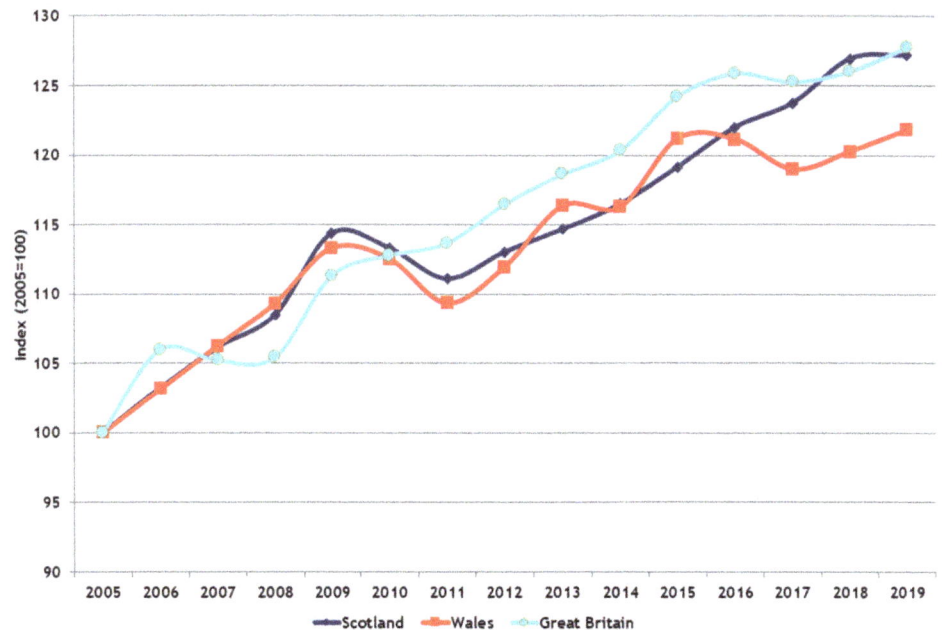

Figure 10-3: Real Term Fares Indices since 2005
Scotland, Wales and Great Britain

Source: Department for Transport Annual Bus Statistics, Sheet BUS0405

Wales. As well as variations in charging levels, the variations also reflect other market differences, most notably in the length of each journey. In London, the typical journey is around 4.4km, compared with 5.7km in the PTE areas, 7.0km in the Shire areas of England and in Scotland, and as high as 8.9km in Wales.

In England, the shape of the graph is very different from the one for fares charged shown in Figure 10-2. The lines are much flatter, showing that despite hefty real-term increases in fares charged, the amount of money paid by each passenger has hardly moved at all – and indeed has fallen in two of the market sectors. Changes in traffic patterns, including the switch to different ticketing products such as day and weekly tickets may account for this, alongside reductions in the reimbursement rates paid by local authorities for concessionary travel.

The analysis shows that bus services in London earned 65.6p per passenger in fares income and concessionary reimbursement from passengers in 2018/19. After allowing for inflation, this figure is 4.9% lower than five years earlier (69.1p) but 4.0% higher than the equivalent

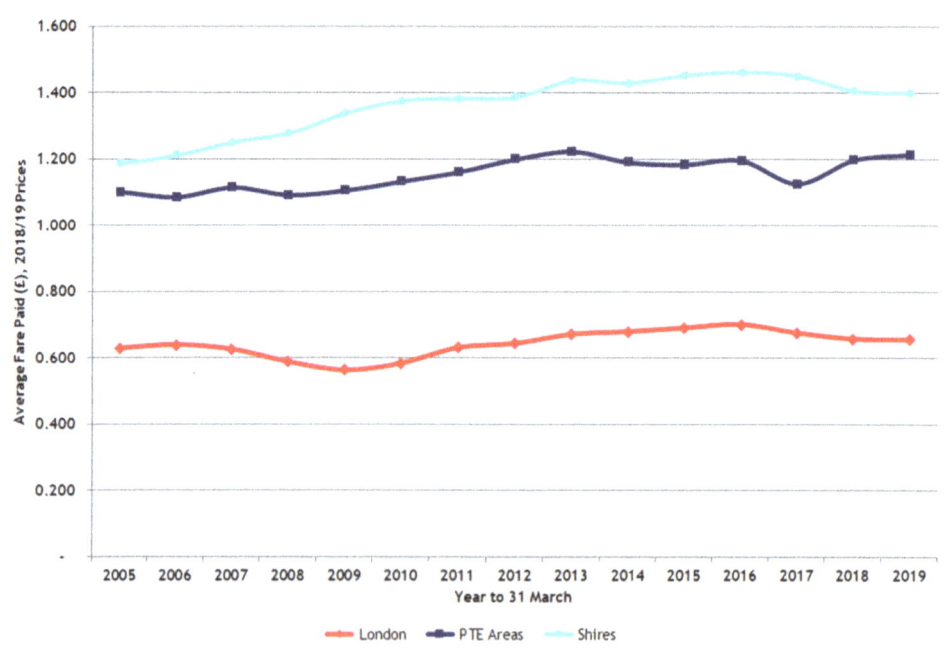

Figure 10-4: Real-Term Movements in Average Fare Paid
London, PTE Areas and English Shires

Figure 10-5: Real-Term Movements in Average Fare Paid
Scotland, Wales and Great Britain

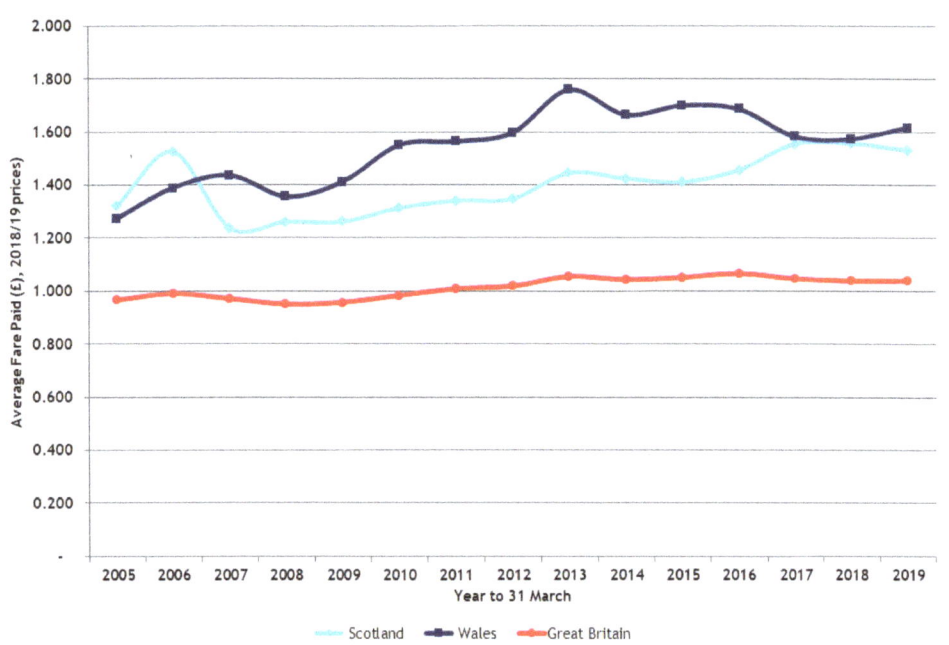

Source: PTIS analysis of data from the Department for Transport Annual Bus Statistics.

in 2004/05 when it was 63.1p.

In the English PTE areas, the earnings per passenger were £1.214 in 2018/19, 2.6% higher than five years earlier, when it stood at £1.184. In 2004/05, the figure was 2.6% lower, at £1.101.

Bus operators in the English Shire areas earned £1.399 per passenger in 2018/19, 3.6% lower than the £1.451 earned five years earlier, but 17.8% ahead of the 2004/05 figure, when it stood at £1.188.

In Scotland, real earnings per passenger journey stood at £1.533 in 2018/19. There was an 8.5% increase over the five year period to 2019, but a fall of 1.6% in 2018/19 itself. Overall, the increase since 2004/05 has been 16.0%.

The Welsh statistics show that real earnings per passenger journey peaked at £1.759 in 2012/13, abut fell back thereafter and stood at £1.617 in 2018/19.

Comparative Travel Costs

It has become the conventional wisdom over the years that the comparative cost of public transport modes has risen against private motoring, resulting in a deterioration in the competitive position of public transport.

However, the revised Consumer Price Indices prepared by the Office of National Statistics back to 1988 tell a somewhat different story[6]. Figure 10-6 illustrates these costs have moved over those 40-plus years. The analysis suggests that the *running costs* have risen by 60.2% over that period, as compared with 61.4% for bus fares and 62.1% for rail fares.

Attempts to increase motoring costs through the fuel duty escalator during the 1990s were abandoned and fuel duty has remained unchanged for several years. At the same time, bus operating costs per passenger have increased and (since 2010 at least) public funding reduced. This has inevitably led to the increases in fares.

Rail fares have faced a similar increase, both as a result of increased operating costs and the decision by successive governments since 2005 to shift the burden of funding the railways from taxpayer to user

Prior to the financial crisis of 2007 and the subsequent recession, the rise in average incomes outstripped all the price increases, so that spending on fares decreased as a proportion of household income. However, falls in average earnings following the recession changed that position, and fares have risen more quickly than incomes, as illustrated by the graph at Figure 10-7 opposite. This has resulted in considerable public dissatisfaction.

---

[6] *Sources for the analysis are ONS Consumer Price Indices. Average income statistics from the Office of National Statistics. Indices used were D7EG Passenger Transport by Road, D7EF Passenger Transport by Railway and D7CP Operation of Personal Transport Equipment. The latter covers spare parts and accessories, fuels and lubricants, maintenance and repairs and "other services". It does not include the purchase of the vehicle itself or insurance. Passenger Transport by Road includes bus, coach and taxi fares.*

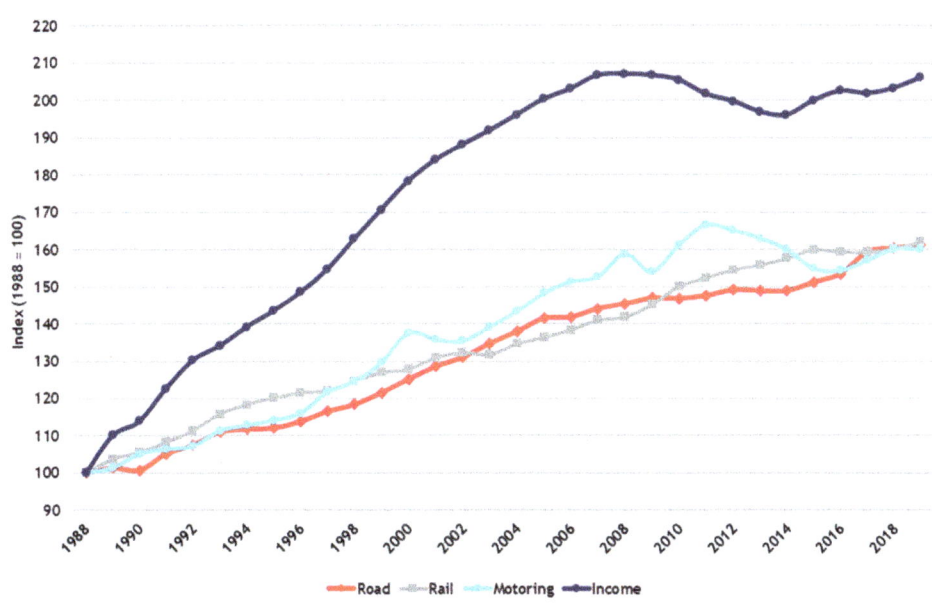

Figure 10-6: Movement in Travel Costs and Average Earnings
In real terms since 1988

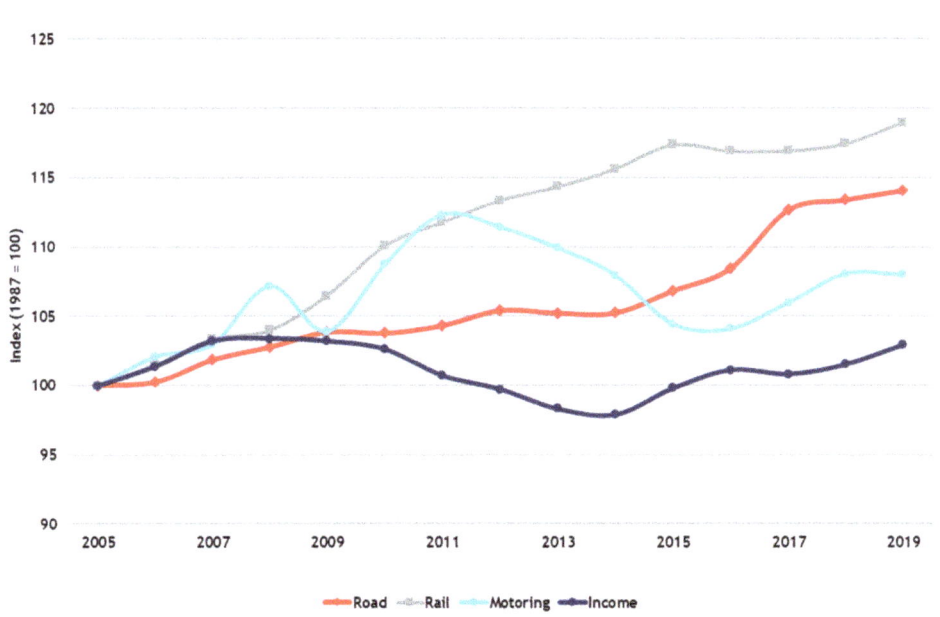

Figure 10-7: Movement in Travel Costs and Average Earnings
In real terms since 2005

Concessionary Travel

Introduction

Concessionary travel has a long history in the UK, dating back to the immediate post-war era in some areas. Free travel was introduced in London as long ago as 1973. The idea is to offer discounted or free travel on public transport modes for certain categories of people – young people, older people and people with some form of illness or disability. The following offers a basic description of how the system works, but more detailed information and guidance is published by Government[7].

By law, operators of registered local bus services are required to accept concessionary passes issued by local authorities and to give the holder a free journey or a discount. The local authority concerned is required to reimburse the operator for that journey.

However, the reimbursement paid is not the full fare that the customer would have paid. This is because the law says that the operator should not benefit financially from the existence of the scheme. This is important, since European regulations prevent concessionary travel schemes from being used to provide hidden subsidy (or state aid) to operators.

It is misleading to suggest, as some do, that concessionary fares reimbursement is a subsidy to bus operators – it is not, and great care is taken to ensure that it is not. The wording enshrined in the 1985 Transport Act is:

> *"It shall be an objective (but not a duty) of an authority when formulating reimbursement arrangements to provide that operators both individually and in the aggregate are financially no better and no worse off as a result of their participation in the scheme to which the arrangements relate."*

---

7   Please see the following:

England. https://www.gov.uk/government/publications/guidance-on-reimbursing-bus-operators-for-concessionary-travel.

Wales: https://gov.wales/topics/transport/public/concessionary/concessionary-travel-guidance/?lang=en

Scotland: https://www.transport.gov.scot/publication/scotland-wide-older-and-disabled-persons-concessionary-bus-scheme-further-reimbursement-research/j260449-04/

The law requires that operators should be reimbursed for:
- Revenue foregone – the fares that would have been paid by passholders who would otherwise have had to pay for their journey
- Net additional costs – extra spending operators needed to accommodate passengers using concessionary passes, including the costs of carrying the extra passengers and administrative costs incurred because of the scheme.

Revenue Foregone

In order to estimate the revenue foregone, two complex calculations are required:
- How many passenger journeys have taken place using the pass that would not have happened if the concession did not exist. These are known as generated journeys.
- What the fare for those journeys would have been had the pass not existed – known as the average fare foregone.

Generated Journeys

Calculating the reimbursement rate requires authorities to estimate the proportion of journeys made by passholders that could be held to have been generated by the scheme (i.e. they would not have taken place if the pass did not exist). This is known as the generation factor and is applied as a percentage to the total number of concessionary journeys that have taken place.

In some areas, it is around 50 years since concessionary schemes were first introduced, so over recent years it has become progressively more difficult to calculate what the "no scheme" scenario would look like. This has resulted to many disagreements between bus companies and local authorities – and an appeals procedure exists to enable disputes to be settled.

Average Fare Foregone

This is not the same as the single fare for the journey, because it is held that:
- some passengers would have bought day tickets or other discounted products

- in the absence of a scheme, operators would develop a promotional strategy including discounts for qualified people.

There are several methods of calculating this figure, depending on the type and frequency of the services being considered.

Net Additional Costs

Operators can claim reimbursement of net additional costs (i.e. after deduction of any revenue generated) under five headings. These are:
- Scheme administration costs
- Marginal operating costs
- Marginal capacity costs
- Peak vehicle requirements
- Other issues – for example the cost of providing larger vehicles than would otherwise be used.

11
Public Spending on Bus Services

Overview

In England, public spending on bus services in 2018/19 totalled £2,024 million. Of this, £1,403 million was spent on services outside London, and £800m in the capital.

In Scotland, spending totalled £314m whilst the Welsh Assembly government spent a further £96m.

This brings the grand total for Great Britain to £2,614m.

The Purpose of the Spending

The spending fell into three broad categories, each of which had a different purpose.
- Tendered Services, via Local Transport Authorities
  - To increase supply by running bus services that the authority considers to be "socially necessary" but which are not commercially viable.
- Support for Bus Services in London, via Transport for London
  - To increase the supply of services and keep fares lower than they would otherwise be.
- BSOG (formerly Fuel Duty Rebate), paid by DfT (England) and Transport Scotland. The grant is called Bus Service Support Grant in Wales and is administered by local authorities. Its purpose is:
  - To increase demand for services by reducing the price
  - To increase supply of services at the margin by reducing the costs of operation.
- Concessionary Fares via Local Authorities
  - To increase demand for services by reducing fares for specified categories of people
  - To deliver social policy objectives in social and health policy.

The amounts of spending in each area of Great Britain are summarised in Table 2 below. The breakdowns by purpose and by geography

Table 2: Public Spending on Bus Services, 2018/19

	Service Support (Net)	Bus Service Operator Grant	Sub-Total Support	Concessionary Fares	Total
London	582	-	582	218	800
PTE Areas	129	85	214	304	518
Shires	264	163	427	458	885
England	975	248	1,223	981	2,204
Scotland	57	55	112	202	314
Wales	26	-	26	70	96
Great Britain	1,058	303	1,361	1,253	2,614
Outside London	476	303	779	1,035	1,813

Source: PTIS consolidation of figures published in Annual Bus Statistics and Transport Statistics Great Britain by Department for Transport plus Scottish and Welsh Transport Statistics.

are illustrated in Figure 11-1 and Figure 11-2 opposite.

It will be seen that none of the three types of expenditure is in truth a subsidy to the operator: public spending on buses involves the purchase of services or tickets by government on behalf of the public.

- The money spent on tendered services represents the purchase from the operator of a particular route or set of departures
- BSOG payments (BSSG in Wales) help to reduce operating costs, therefore increasing supply at the margin and keeping fares lower than they otherwise would be.
- The concessionary travel payments represent Government buying discounted travel from the operators for certain sections of the population (see section . above for a further discussion of this).

Originally, BSOG in its days as Fuel Duty Rebate represented revenue foregone by government rather than a subsidy. This is the way in which it was defined between 1965 and 2000.

Payment for concessionary travel is reimbursement to operators for revenue foregone – fares that would otherwise be paid by the travelling public if the concessionary pass did not exist. Concessionary travel is a subsidy to the *pass holder*, not to the bus operator.

EU regulations were stringent, and prevented concessionary reim-

Figure 11-1: Public Spending on Bus Services in 2018/19 by purpose

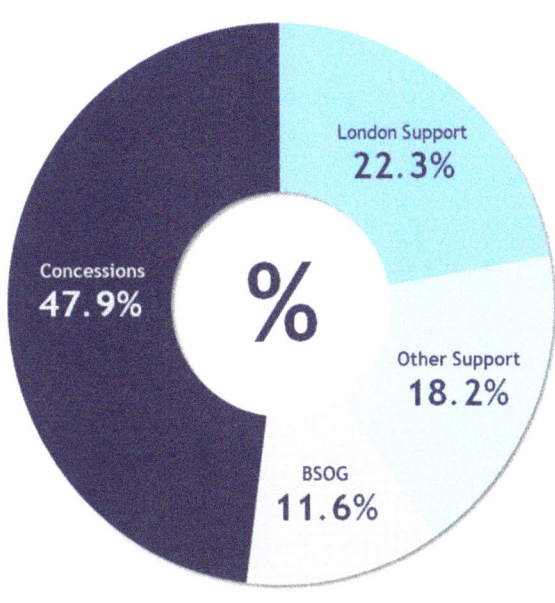

Figure 11-2: Public Spending on Bus Services in 2018/19 by area/nation

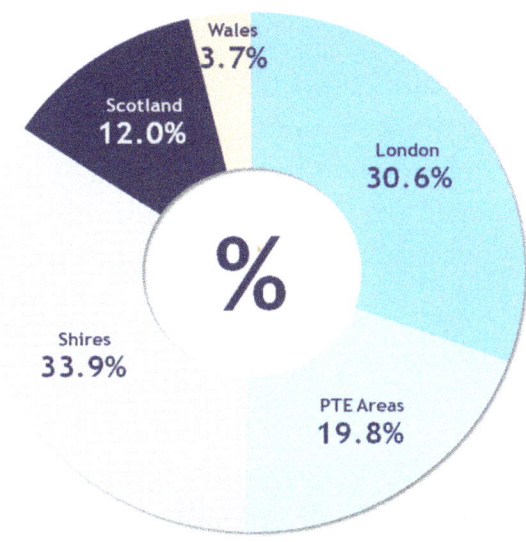

Source for Figs 11-1 and 11-2: PTIS consolidation of figures published in Annual Bus Statistics by Department for Transport plus Scottish and Welsh Transport Statistics.

bursement from being used as a form of state aid. Operators are not therefore reimbursed for the full cost of any journey, since a proportion of trips by pass holders are held to be generated by the existence of the scheme (see Chapter 10). In 2018/19, for example, reimbursement per concessionary journey was £1.12 in England outside London[8] compared with an average fare paid by paying passengers of £1.34 – a reduction of 17%.

Benchmarking Spending

Introduction

There are two possible ways of benchmarking expenditure – by passenger journey and by resident population. Each method has its advantages:
- Spend per head of the population might be held to measure the inputs, possibly a good way of testing the "fairness" of the spend in different communities – though of course such a judgement also needs consider differing priorities in different parts of the country.
- Spend per passenger journey effectively measures the out-turn cost in terms of what 'value' the community has received for its money.

The following sections look at and comment upon each of the two measures, again looking at both purpose and geography.

Spend per Capita

The numbers for this measure are shown in Figure 11-3, which illustrates the wide variation in spending levels per head of the population between the different market segments. London spends the most, by a very wide margin, at £89. Next closest is Scotland on £57. The PTE areas spend £43 whilst Wales spends £30 and the English Shire areas £25.

Spending per Passenger Journey

Overall, this analysis, shown at Figure 11-4, suggests that levels of expenditure and support per passenger journey are roughly in line with what might be expected, with costs per passenger being higher in the

---

[8] Source: Department for Transport Concessionary Fares Statistics BUS0830. The average fare quoted is estimated by PTIS from data in DfT Annual Bus Statistics. Since this also includes child fares, the actual discount to the average adult fare will be higher than the 17%.

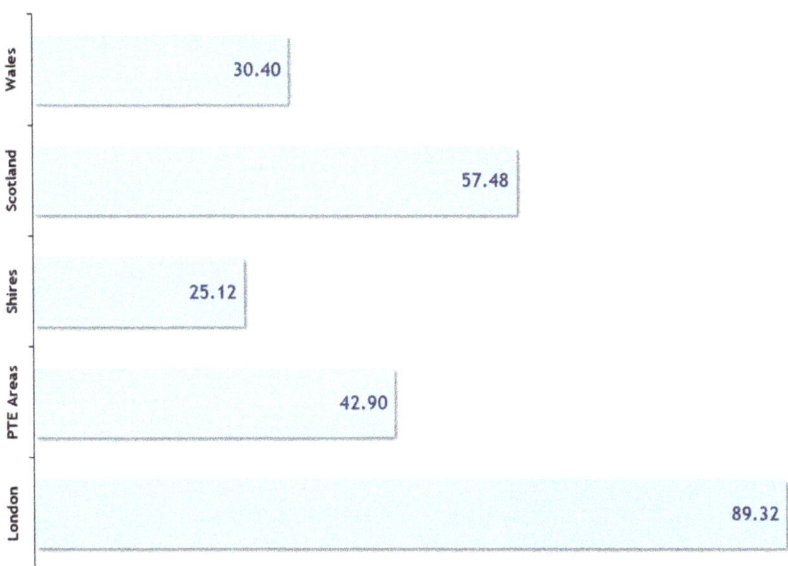

Figure 11-3: Spending Per Capita on Bus Services 2018/19

- Wales: 30.40
- Scotland: 57.48
- Shires: 25.12
- PTE Areas: 42.90
- London: 89.32

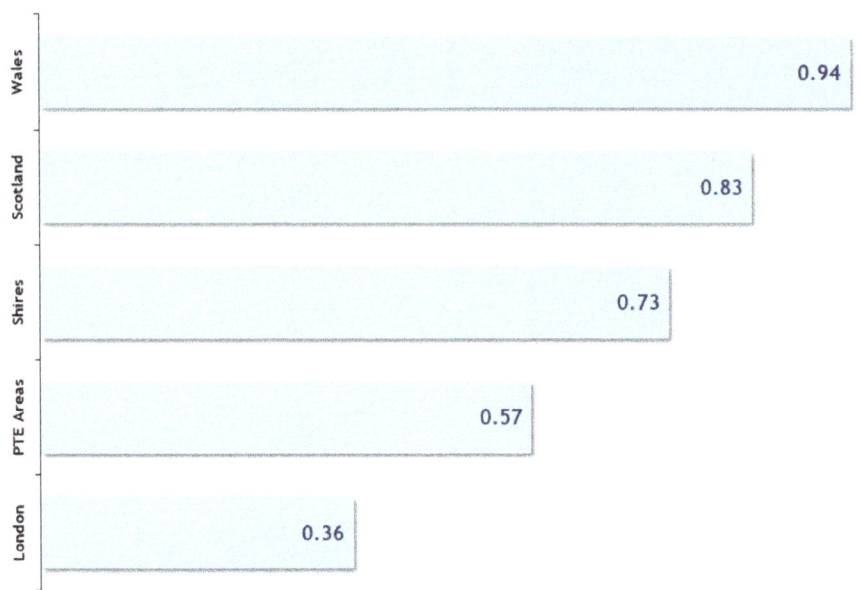

Figure 11-4: Spending per Passenger Journey on Bus Services 2018/19

- Wales: 0.94
- Scotland: 0.83
- Shires: 0.73
- PTE Areas: 0.57
- London: 0.36

Source for Figs 11-3 and 11-4: PTIS analysis of Annual Bus Statistics DfT, Scottish Transport Statistics, Welsh Transport Statistics. Population Data from ONS Mid-Year Estimates 2019 more rural areas – reflecting lower volumes and longer journeys.

Thus, the highest levels of support per passenger in 2016/17 were in Wales, at 94p. Scotland came next at 83p, followed by the English Shires on 75p. In the more urban PTE Areas, support was much lower at 57p, whilst London's network cost 36p for each passenger journey.

Changes in Spending Patterns

Since 2010, there have been major cuts in spending on bus services – as in most areas of public expenditure. After adjusting for inflation, the total fell by £707m (27%) per annum between 2010/11 and 2018/19. The chart at Figure 11-5 below tracks the changes in real total spending outside London since 2004/05, comparing these numbers with snapshots from 1986 and 1996. The low point occurred in 1995/96, when spending had been cut back to £1,522m in today's money. By 2010/11, this had risen by almost a billion pounds to £2,413m. That proved to be the high watermark, and the total fell rapidly to £1,821m in 2018/19. Further cuts were expected, until Covid-19 upended everything.

12
Looking Ahead

Covid-19 and the Future

At the start of 2020, reports began to circulate of a mysterious illness in an little-known province of China. Within weeks, the illness, now known as Covid-19, had swept the world and turned everything - economics, social life, transport - on its head.

As the infection spread, demand for public transport started to fall. Even before the lockdown, bus passenger numbers had fallen to just above half of normal, according to DfT Statistics[9]. The imposition of the lockdown in the third week of March 2020 drove passenger numbers down to between 12 and 17 per cent of the previous year's levels. After

---

9   Transport Use during the Coronavirous Covid-19 Pandemic, DfT, published weekly since March 2020

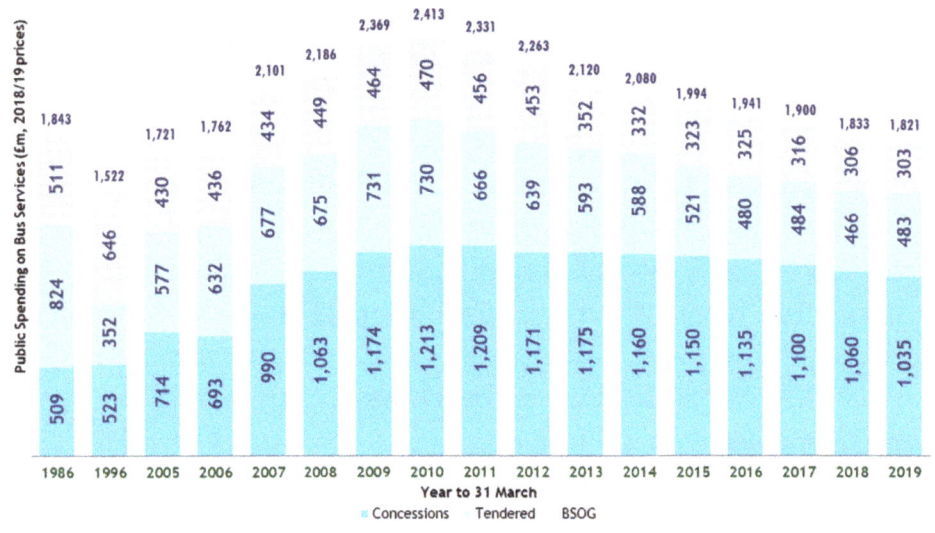

Figure 11-5: Trends in Public Spending on Bus Services
Great Britain outside London since 1986, Constant (2018/19) Prices

Source: PTIS analysis of Annual Bus Statistics DfT, Scottish Transport Statistics, Welsh Transport Statistics.

the initial few weeks, numbers started to rise again as the economy was opened up during the summer, but fell back as restrictions were progressively tightened during the autumn, culminating in the second and third lockdowns. However, the loss of patronage did not go as far as it had done in those early weeks of the crisis, bottoming out at around one-third of previous demand in London and 25-28 per cent outside the capital. The overall trends are illustrated in Figure 12-1 overleaf.

In response to these falls, the government introduced Covid Bus Service Support Grant (CBSSG) in March 2020 to assist bus operators outside London in running networks agreed with the local authorities in their area. In addition, financial assistance has been provided to Transport for London to keep the bus network running.

A year on from the start of the process, it is clear that the impact of the pandemic will be severe and long-lasting, affecting the economy, and consequently on the demand for transport. There will also be an impact on government finances which could also affect the bus industry in the years to come.

In trying to assess the medium to long term consequences of virus crisis on bus demand, there are likely to be three overlapping drivers of change. They are:
- Social distancing
- Lifestyle Changes
- The Economy

Social Distancing

As happened in the summer of 2020, the lifting of restrictions on shopping, hospitality venues and other attractions is likely to be accompanied by continuing requirements of mask-wearing and social distancing, which reduces public transport capacity significantly. Those who are obliged to travel to and from work may prefer to do so in their own car rather than sharing space on public transport or in a taxi. There is already evidence of this happening as travel by car recovered more quickly and to higher levels each time the restrictions were lifted. Further evidence of this came in research by Transport Focus, published at the beginning of April 2021, which showed that only 37% of current non-users regarded bus travel as safe from Covid. This number was, though, in stark contrast to

Figure 12-1: Bus Use during Covid

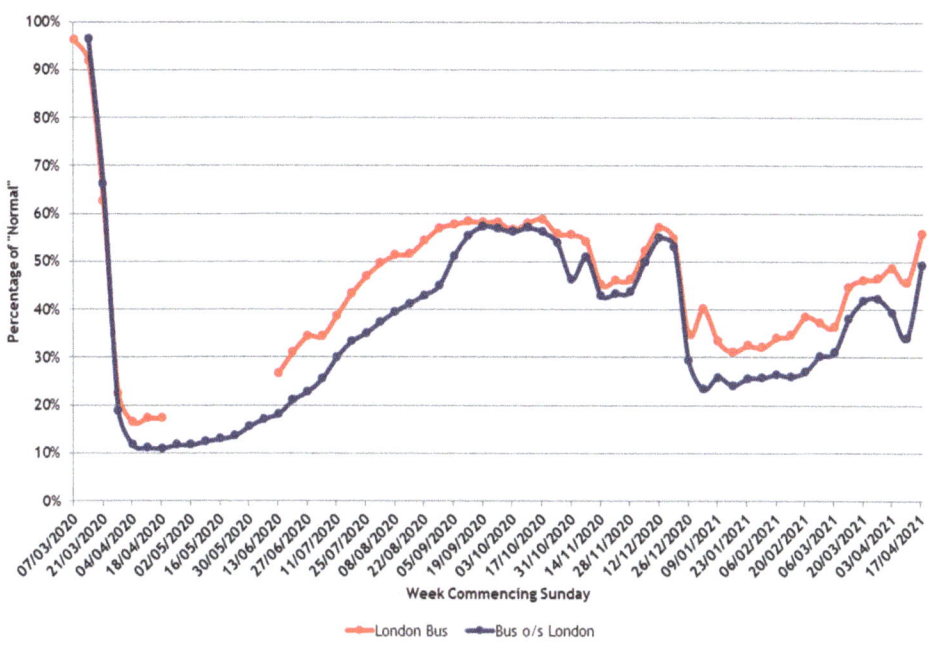

Source: PTIS Analysis of Transport Use during the Coronavirus Covid-19 Pandemic, DfT, published weekly since March 2020. No figures for London are available between early April and mid-June 2020, as fare collection was suspended during this period to protect staff from infection

the 84% of *users* who felt safe from Covid using the bus. Government advice, still encouraging people to avoid public transport in mid-April 2021, would also need to change to assist any revival.

Even as the vaccination programme proceeds, this phase is likely to last several months. Meanwhile, alterations to behaviour and the economic consequences of the crisis have already started to play out.

Lifestyle Changes

It is widely expected that some of the habits forced on people during the crisis will continue after it is over – especially where these merely accelerated trends that were already under way. These changes are likely to affect all journey purposes:
- Work – more home working and video conferencing, resulting in fewer commuting and business trips
- Shopping – more online shopping resulting in fewer trips and more closures, making high streets less attractive

- Leisure – more home entertainment and streaming, home food deliveries – resulting in fewer trips to theatre, cinema, restaurants and possibly sporting venues.
- Personal business – acceleration of the move of financial services transactions online, coupled with a similar move to remote consultations and diagnostics in the NHS. Both might be expected to reduce demand for personal business and escort trips.
- Education – a move to more online teaching may be accelerated, driven both by demand and the need to cut premises costs.

The Economy

There is little consensus amongst economists as to the nature and extent of the damage that the crisis will have to done to the economy. Some argue that there will be a quick bounce back to activity levels seen before the lockdown; others suggest long-lasting damage. There is a consensus that public spending will be under pressure and that higher taxation is likely to be necessary to service and repay the huge debts that will have been incurred.

Summary

Looking again at the five principal purposes for travel by bus, it is possible to identify the threats to each:
- Work and Business – fewer jobs and lower prosperity will impact on the number of commuting and business trips
- Leisure – lower disposable income may be expected to reduce travel demand
- Shopping – reduced footfall as volumes fall and as shop closures make High Streets less attractive places to visit
- Personal – pressure on costs will drive more branches in financial services to close, so reinforcing the trend to drive financial services, legal services and some medical work online.
- Education – spending cuts and reduced demand lead to reducing numbers of students and fewer university places.

The expectation must be that a combination of some or all these movements could have serious consequences for the current level of demand for bus travel. Given the nature of the business and the marginal nature of much of its existing level of supply, further service cuts or fare increases would be inevitable without continued government intervention.

As a rough guide, using the journey purpose numbers, outline calculations on a set of "reasonable" forward assumptions for each journey purpose suggests that a period of social distancing could be expected to run at around 55% to 60% below previous demand levels (in line with summer and autumn 2020), whilst a return to "normal" would be at a level between 18 and 26 per cent lower than before the lockdown. Even getting to those levels would depend crucially on the extent and speed of the recovery in the wider economy.

De-carbonising Transport

As has already been seen, demand for transport, as measured by the Government in passenger kilometres, had reached a new peak in 2019, totalling 873 billion. This was the last year for which figures were available at the time of writing. 84.5% of that demand was met by private car, van and taxi, making a total of 738 billion passenger kilometres. This compared with 32.6 billion for buses and coaches.

At that time, it was still expected that there would be a continued long-term growth in car ownership and use, with a consequent rise in the level of road traffic. This had been given expression in the 2018 National Road Traffic Forecast, which envisaged growth of between 17% and 51% between a base year of 2015 and 2050.

There was much concern amongst policy-makers that the Government was facing both ways - promoting zero carbon emissions by 2050 in the knowledge that the achievement of such a target would require a significant modal shift away from the car towards active travel and public transport, as well as electrification of the vehicle fleet.

This was highlighted in the government's consultation document, *Decarbonising Transport – Setting the Challenge*, which was published in March 2020, just as the coronavirus crisis was taking hold.

One of the six strands set out in the document concerned "accelerating modal shift to public and active transport". Under that, there were four objectives, which were:

- Help make public transport and active travel the natural first choice for daily activities
- Support fewer car trips through a coherent, convenient and cost-effective public network; and explore how we might use cars differently in future
- Encourage cycling and walking for short journeys
- Explore how to best support the behaviour change required.

Later in the document, the Department restates modal shift as one of its priorities:

"Accelerating modal shift to public and active transport:

"We want public transport and active travel to be the natural first choice for our daily activities. An important aspect of reducing emissions from transport will be to use our cars less and be able to rely on a convenient, cost-effective and coherent public transport network. For those able to do so, we would like cycling and walking to be the easy and obvious choice for short journeys. We are already exploring how we can use vehicles differently, such as through shared mobility. New technologies and business models may help facilitate modal shift, such as Mobility as a Service platforms. This will require behavioural changes and we will consider how government and others can support this shift through infrastructure and encouraging those forms of travel."

More detail on how the government's proposals for the delivery of improvements came in March 2021, with the publication of a National Bus Strategy, *Bus Back Better*. This set out new requirements for local transport authorities to deliver Bus Service Improvement Plans, working in partnership with local operators under the Enhanced Partnership framework set out in the Bus Services Act 2017. There will be an expectation that bus priority measures will be more widely introduced, alongside low-carbon vehicles powered by electricity or hydrogen. The government has promised £3 billion in additional funding over the life of the current Parliament. Reform of Bus Service Operators' Grant (BSOG) and a review of concessionary fares funding were also promised.

It has to be remembered, though, that achieving modal shift is not easy and there is a need to grasp the scale of the change needed. With the volume for travel by car exceeding bus by a factor of more than ten, any switch from car to bus has a major effect on the latter.

Each one per cent travelled by car represents 7.4 billion passenger kilometres. Since only 32.6 billion passenger km were travelled by bus and coach in 2019, an extra 7.4 billion would represent 22% of existing demand. The same figure for the railways would be 11%.

We can thus estimate by how much demand for public transport needs to increase if significant modal shift were to be achieved. The figures are illustrated in the chart at Figure 12-2 below. As can be seen, numbers are challenging, not to say daunting.

On the buses, the early stages of a major shift could be accommodated by increasing average loads on existing vehicles. Extensive use of priority measures and a reduction in traffic could free bus services from congestion, so boosting the capacity of the existing fleet through better utilisation. Some operators have suggested in the past that this could increase capacity in urban areas by 10 per cent or more.

Once that resource had been exhausted, expansion of services and fleets would be required - with huge increases in the demand for labour. The results would also be immense in terms of the increases that would

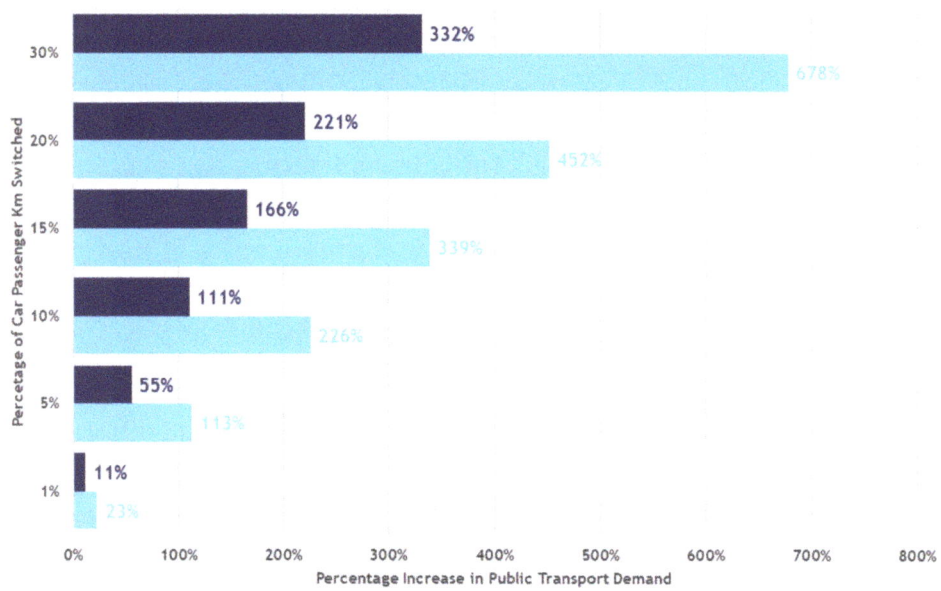

Source: PTIS Analysis. Figures based on Transport Statistics Great Britain 2020, Sheet TSGB0101

be needed. This would include new vehicles (or old ones retained for longer), funding requirements and additional staff and management.

Staffing is crucial and will strike a particular chord with managers who have had to deal with past staff shortages in many parts of the country. These have been very difficult, as the resulting inability to provide a reliable service does severe harm to the market position of the bus. Expansion on a large scale would undoubtedly exacerbate recruitment difficulties.

This does not mean that the industry could not cope with expansion – especially bearing in mind the falls in average load discussed earlier, and the significant expansion achieved in London before and after the introduction of congestion charging. However, it would not necessarily be a simple matter, even if the public consent or the political will existed to implement the measures necessary to achieve such a major shift.

Conclusions

As mentioned in the introduction, this book set out to provide an overview of how buses work. The aim was to provide enough knowledge and understanding to enable the non-specialist to appreciate the key drivers of cost, profitability and demand in the bus industry.

We set out to look at:
- the level of and changes in operating costs
- the level of – and need for – operator profits
- the speed and reliability of bus services
- volumes of demand, which influence operating cost per passenger
- demographic influences on bus demand
- competition from the private car and other modes of transport
- competition from other bus operators.

The work has been derived from the more detailed analysis we have undertaken over the last 30 years, which is still available online and in a series of more detailed reports.

There are several factors which make the bus industry unique, and set particular challenges for its managers:
- The instantly perishable nature of the product
- The high proportion of total costs represented by labour costs

- The fact that operators are not in control of key aspects of their business, namely:
  - Operating environment – speed and reliability are heavily influenced by other traffic
  - Point of sale – stops and terminals are run by third parties (usually local authorities)
  - Staff productivity – heavily influenced by speed and therefore congestion.

Competition from other modes, particularly the private car, is a key influence in the market place, and influences operators' policies and marketing strategies. Success in bus operation in the UK over the last two decades has come where operators, in partnership with local authorities, have pursued the twin goals of high-quality service delivery and public policies designed to encourage and promote bus use. These typically including parking policy, bus priorities and other motoring charges such as a workplace parking levy or road pricing. Such policies have encouraged people to use the bus largely because they have re-balanced the generalised costs of bus and car journeys.

We saw these policies in action in London for many years and a range of other towns and cities around the country, including Brighton, Cambridge, Edinburgh, Oxford, Nottingham and Reading. It is not difficult to do – though it may be politically extremely challenging at times. It is no accident, though, that this is the model which the government is seeking to adopt across other authorities in its National Bus Strategy. However, there is no 'magic wand' that can be waived to solve local transport problems.

Ultimately, the inescapable reality is that society must pay the cost of providing the level of bus services it requires. There are only two sources of revenue – the customer and the taxpayer. One or other must meet the costs of provision – including the cost of the capital needed – or services must be reduced to the levels which are affordable or commercially viable. There is no easy solution to these issues, and to pretend otherwise is to mislead policymakers and the electorate.

Get a fresh angle on the big picture in passenger transport

PASSENGER TRANSPORT MONITOR

Independent Analysis and Commentary since 1991

A track record of insight

One of the UK's most experienced business analysis services for transport operators, providing knowledge, understanding and comment since 1991.

Products available:
- Online Subscriptions
- Report Sales
- Finances & Markets
- Bespoke Analysis

Modes covered:
- UK Rail
- UK Bus
- UK Rapid Transit

GIVE US A CLICK!
www.passtrans.co.uk

Visit our web site to subscribe, buy our reports, read our commentaries or ask us for help

Alternatively, you can e-mail us at admin@passtrans.co.uk, or telephone us on 01729 840756.
You can write to us at:
83 Latimer Road, Eastbourne, East Sussex, BN22 7EL.

www.ingramcontent.com/pod-product-compliance
Lightning Source LLC
Chambersburg PA
CBHW041958080526
44588CB00021B/2783